Wh ook:

"This is composer
seeking

— *glected Art*

"*From* n-scoring
techniq e field of
scoring verything
from th

Institute

"With ith a little
help fr imply an
outstan who want
to see t arts."
nd Reviews

"This working
professi e process
of creat ising with
confide

University

"*From* w into an
industry nposer."

University

from SCORE to SCREEN
Sequencers, Scores, & Second Thoughts
The New Film Scoring Process
Sonny Kompanek

SCHIRMER
TRADE
BOOKS

New York / London / Paris / Sydney / Tokyo / Berlin / Copenhagen / Madrid

Schirmer Trade Books
A Division of Music Sales Corporation, New York

Exclusive Distributors:
Music Sales Corporation
257 Park Avenue South, New York, NY 10010 USA
Music Sales Limited
8/9 Firth Street, London W1D 3JB England
Music Sales Pty. Limited
120 Rothschild Street, Rosebery, Sydney, NSW 2018, Australia

Order No. SCH 10148
International Standard Book Number: 0-8256-7308-9

Printed in the United States of America
By Vicks Lithograph and Printing Corporation

Library of Congress Cataloging-in-Publication Data

Kompanek, Sonny.
 From score to screen : sequencers, scores, and second thoughts : the new film scoring process / by Sonny
Kompanek.
 p. cm.
 Includes bibliographical references.
 ISBN 0-8256-7308-9 (pbk. : alk. paper)
 1. Motion picture music—Instruction and study. 2. Instrumentation and orchestration—Instruction and study. 3.
Composition (Music) 4. Music—Vocational guidance. I. Title.
MT64.M65K65 2004
781.5'4213—dc22
 2004008839

Contents

Acknowledgments

I want to acknowledge my faithful readers whose thoughtful comments were essential to making this text as easy to read and useful as possible: Lee Norris, James Oakar, Michael Rusz, and most of all my wife Elissa and son Chris. Also, a special thanks to Chris McGlumphy.

In addition, I am especially grateful to the following for the benefit of their friendship and experience over the years: Kenny Ascher, Roger Blanc, Nat Brooks, Carter Burwell, Emile Charlap, Gary Chester, Ed Choi, Michael Farrow, Alan Foust, Vic Fraser, Todd Kasow, David Matthews, Lee Norris, Jim Pugh, Ron Sadoff, Michael Small, Adam Smalley, Bill Waranoff, and Jim White.

And finally, a big thanks to Andrea Rotondo for her unwavering enthusiasm and support from day one, and her hard work in making this book successful.

Credits

Managing Editor: Andrea M. Rotondo
Technical Editor: Tom Kenny
Copyeditor: Barbara Schultz
Proofreader: Amy Blankstein
Cover Design: Phil Gambrill
Production Director: Dan Earley
Interior Designer: Len Vogler
Publicity Coordinator: Alison M. Wofford

About the author

*S*onny Kompanek has orchestrated more than 60 major feature films (including *De-lovely, The Alamo, The Rookie, Conspiracy Theory, Hudsucker Proxy, It Could Happen To You, Rob Roy,* and *Barton Fink*), TV productions (including *Sex & the City, Nero Wolfe, Witness to the Mob,* and *South Pacific*), and artist arrangements for Wynton Marsalis, Wyclef Jean, Boyz II Men, Soul Asylum, and Victor Borge. Kompanek has taught at various music schools, including the Eastman School of Music, Mannes College of Music, and currently New York University. He lives in New York with his wife, Elissa, son, Chris, and daughter, Nina.

Foreword

This is an invaluable and extremely important book for any aspiring composer seeking a career as a film composer. Sonny Kompanek brings long experience at the highest levels of his profession as an orchestrator for feature films and arranger for some of the world's leading musicians. As a supervising music editor for many mainstream (and a few not-so-mainstream) feature films, I have worked with numerous composers in the circumstances Sonny so ably describes and elucidates in this book. Even so, I was delighted to find myself learning something new on almost every page of *From Score to Screen*.

The author's approach to his subject is comprehensive. He deftly explains the "how to" of every aspect of his craft while also providing equally critical insights into the handling of the many inter-personal relationships encountered by the composer in the film-scoring process. I once had a piano teacher tell me, "Talent is the cheapest commodity," meaning one needs many other personal attributes in addition to talent to make it in the professional world. This Sonny knows and makes clear: That *how* the film composer interacts with these individuals is *at least* as important as what the composer will write for the film. In addition, and just as crucially, he provides advice on how best to handle the many pitfalls that can be encountered dealing with high-powered talent and large egos.

From Score to Screen shines in all its aspects: An astute look at each professional individual one encounters in the process of creating a film score (orchestrator, conductor, musicians, director, music editor, mixer, contractor and copyist) and how best to utilize their special talents and expertise; networking and self-promotion; improving your skills as a composer; working with both MIDI sequences and live orchestra (including such valuable information as what MIDI can do—as well as what it *cannot* do); creating the right ensemble for the score, running a recording session, fixing problem passages and much, much more. The "Resource" section at the back of the book will prove priceless to anyone just beginning to learn the film-scoring business.

What inhabits every page of Sonny's book is that rare quality so seldom found in writers and teachers of any profession: An affection not only for his subject, but for informing and helping the student eventually achieve a success equal to his own. This unselfish willingness to share his vast experience with others is what sets this book apart from so many others.

There has long been a need for a book such as *From Score to Screen* and Sonny has, with skill and intelligence, more than filled that need. I'm sure it will be the benchmark for books of this genre for the foreseeable future.

Roy M. Prendergast
Los Angeles, CA

ABOUT ROY PRENDERGAST

Mr. Prendergast, author of the venerable text *Film Music: A Neglected Art,* holds an undergraduate degree in piano and a graduate degree in composition. After serving on the faculty of the School of Music at the University of North Carolina at Greensboro, he moved to Los Angeles where he has been working as a music editor in the motion picture industry, primarily in Los Angeles and London, since 1979. He has numerous television series, movies, and mini-series credits, including *The Day After,* for which he received his first of two Emmy Awards. He is also a member of the Motion Picture Academy of Arts and Sciences.

He has edited music for over 35 feature films, many with the Scottish composer, Patrick Doyle. Mr. Prendergast's credits include *Caddyshack, Dead Again, Sense and Sensibility, A Little Princess, Much Ado About Nothing, Carlito's Way, Indochine, Shakespeare in Love, East/West* as well as the less serious, *Road Trip* and *Tomcats.* His more recent credits include *Tears of the Sun, Terminator 3,* and *The Clearing.*

Mr. Prendergast has lectured on film music in many venues including Sydney and Melbourne, Australia, the Eastman School of Music, and Oxford University. His work has taken him to every major film-scoring center in the world, including Los Angeles, New York, Melbourne, London, Munich, Vienna, Warsaw, Prague, and Toronto—not to mention more out-of-the-way venues such as Seattle, Washington and Sofia, Bulgaria.

*I*ntroduction

*W*e are in a filmmaking explosion. What used to be a highly technical process involving a knowledge of cameras, lighting, and equipment has now been simplified to a "My First Sony" level for the general public. The basics are so simple that anyone with a digital video camera and a computer can begin to make films, edit them, and copy them to DVD. The tools to do this are even included as standard equipment on new computers. Also, there are more books, magazines, Web sites, and courses of study on filmmaking than ever before. The HBO program *Project Greenlight*, which documents a winning screenwriter and director as they make their first million-dollar film, boasts more than 7,000 applicants. From my first-hand experience as a teacher, universities that have filmmaking departments fill their enrollment quotas faster than any other. Creative writing departments are adding screenwriting to their course offerings, and some even offer it as a major.

With so much filmmaking comes so much film scoring. Not too many years ago, both the making and scoring of films were the province of those fortunate few who lived in major cities and had connections. Now films are made and scored everywhere, and composers of every kind are getting into the act—classical, rap, pop, even refugees from the techno-synth world who, without sequencing software, might not be making music at all. It is, after all, the computer's capability of emulating live instruments and synchronizing with film that has made film scoring a real hands-on medium. No longer is scoring an exotic process done in some faraway place only by music-schooled "score-writing types" who have an inordinate number of live musicians at their disposal. Directors everywhere can hear their synth mockups instantly, and the composer can be the kid down the street.

Curiously, even with all of the technical advances in the filmmaking process, it is the sound of the live symphony orchestra that is, after all these years, still the primary sound medium for most Hollywood film scores. That monolithic purveyor of pop culture, the major film studio, has been able to provide the big budgets necessary to fund the big scores, and even when the budgets are lower (as with independent filmmakers), we find composers emulating the big orchestral sound using fewer live musicians, but supported by synthesizers. Fortunately, it is still easier, more cost-effective, and more desirable to have a live orchestra do "another take with more of a smile" than to emulate such a change on just a synth, and any fears we might have had of the synths monopolizing the process have long since dissipated.

Ironically, while symphonic orchestras everywhere are experiencing diminishing audiences (except perhaps in larger metropolitan areas), the sound of the orchestra, for the most part, seems to have found a happy home in the film world. And, with classical music in general being shoved to the sidelines of our culture, out of earshot of anyone who is not in active pursuit, the movie theater is probably the one remaining place where the general public hears anything remotely resembling classical music performed on a great sound system. Due to the long-standing neglect of our public music education system, increased budget cuts for many years have meant decreased arts funding for our schools, and some children become adults without knowing the existence of any music beyond what pop culture puts in their ears at every turn, from radio stations to clothing stores to pop tune promotions on the Internet.

A true story illustrates my point:

In New York there used to be a separate store for classical music as part of J&R Music World. I overheard a young woman asking a sales person for a pop CD; he replied that this was the *classical* store, and she would have to go to the *pop* store a few doors down the street. Again she asked for her pop CD, and again the salesperson said she was in the wrong store. She clearly did not understand what he was talking about and finally wandered out complaining how stupid the salesperson was. To her, every store that sold CDs carried the same thing. Sadly, her misconception has, for the most part, become the norm.

I am reminded of this situation again when I see young film directors who seem to have had little experience listening to symphonic music. They have apparently grown up in a musical world consisting of only rock, punk, rap, etc. and seem to be unaware of any orchestral film scores along the way. One of the directors I am thinking of came to a recording session and asked, after a 70-piece orchestra had just played the first cue, "What was that?" The composer was dumbfounded (hadn't the director heard the synth mockups?). The director then requested something more like the temp track, which consisted mainly of guitars and drums.

To counteract this lack of musical awareness among young film directors, common sense would dictate that film schools should encourage their student directors to work with nearby music school students, thereby nurturing a mutual learning process. Composers need to gain experience with the dramatic language of directors, and directors can observe the process of writing and rewriting a film score through synth mockups, becoming familiar with the many ways a score can enhance a film. Inter-departmental relationships like this are, unfortunately, more the exception than the rule.

This relatively new film scoring process, shared between the composer and director—a trial-and-error, back-and-forth, computer-based approach to scoring—allows the director's input for every cue in the score. It has come about over the past 20 years and is now so standard that I doubt any young film composer could get started today without it. The days of a director not hearing the score until the recording session (and being surprised, for better or worse) are over. Until now, the score was created first and the *sound* came later, with only the composer and orchestrator knowing for sure what was coming. Today, the opposite is true, with the sound coming first and the printed score later. The composer illustrates his musical intent with a sequencer, the director watches, listens, and offers his criticism (and eventual approval), after which the score and parts for live musicians are prepared. This book was conceived to bring this process home to students—to give young film composers insight into the sometimes exhausting, but nonetheless necessary, process of altering their scores for a director.

Almost all of my film-scoring students at NYU use sequencers to create their scores. Our talk mainly focuses on what they have already composed, not what to do before they score. We may cite existing film scores for insight into certain techniques, but we mainly spot a cue together, as they would with a director. Then, after they have written music to the film, I play devil's advocate (or disgruntled director) and ask for changes or new versions to be written for the same cue. This is the way the real-life process works. The difference is the length of the film, ours being from one to eight minutes.

And so, this book is not a history of film scoring or a how-to book for creating a film score. Rather, the focus is on the many things you will have to do with your score *after* it exists, from changing it to please a director to recording it in the studio. Most crafty musicians interested in film can create a computer-sequenced score of some kind for a director to hear. From that point until the score reaches the screen is an area about which most students of film composition are unfamiliar because such things are learned over time, from project to project.

How to interpret a director's criticism, how to translate your MIDI files into a printed score for live musicians, how to fix your score on the spot, how to increase or decrease elements of motion and tension—these and other things we will explore on the road *from score to screen.*

Author's note: Throughout this book I use the pronoun "he" for simplicity's sake. There are, of course, as many talented female composers as there are male.

The cast

When a composer sits down to create a film score, an amazing process takes place. The essence of a film is translated into musical themes and gestures that, in turn, become dramatic elements in themselves for the audience to experience. These musical elements can reinforce what is seen on the screen or play against it for contrast. By creating musical themes that work in a variety of dramatic settings over the course of the film, the composer can enhance or even manipulate our interpretation of characters, moods, or events. By virtue of its style and dramatic structure, the music leaves emotional trails, non-verbal threads, weaving in and out of the film's fabric, making connections in ways that can be unique to each film. And the composer is able to do all of this with the "help" of a director and producers looking over his shoulder. In as little as three to six weeks an entire score can be created in and around a barrage of meetings and phone calls.

If the recording sessions can be booked a week apart, there is time to record, write, record, write, etc., but that doesn't happen very often because the music comes at the end of the post-production phase, with little time for such a leisurely schedule. I have never heard of a film studio telling a composer, "Let us know when you're finished writing the music and we'll book the recording time." In order to meet often fast-approaching deadlines, additional help is available to the composer in the form of a music editor, orchestrator, mixer, contractor, and copyist, all of whom are quite used to the inevitable time squeeze.

THE COMPOSER

Film composers have extremely diverse talents. Some are technophiles; others don't even own a computer. Some went to music school and play an instrument well; others barely read music and don't really have a performing instrument. But all are capable of producing unique film scores in their own ways. Andre Previn, in his book *No Minor Chords*, mentions that he once found himself orchestrating for a composer who could only thump out a melody with his thumb, the author filling in the rest. Good sources of insight into the idiosyncrasies of different composers and their wide-ranging approaches to film scoring can be found in interviews, which are available on the Net, or in books and magazines.

It is helpful for beginning film score composers to realize that they do not have to fit into a type or even have a formal music education. (Some film composers don't even like watching films.) Presumably, of course, the more you study the better your music will be and the easier it might be to compose with flexibility in a variety of settings, but there is a paradox that can come into play. A well-schooled composer can sometimes have difficulty composing music other than the "stand-alone" variety, which always takes center stage. Then, only making matters worse, he cannot change a note for fear of upsetting the musicality of it all. If, upon playing your music to film people, you often get the comment, "That was a great piece of music, but...," you might be one of these composers. Consider the following traits common to many film score composers I have known and see if they fit you.

1. A "filmic vision": People often say to you, "That really works well with the film."

2. Willingness to rewrite or change your music many times at the request of someone whose musical taste you may not respect.

3. Perseverance and determination to work all hours until a cue is "right," not needing a lot of sleep.

4. Crafty, inventive, goes for an unusual way of solving a musical problem.

5. Can communicate with a director in dramatic (not musical) terms.

6. Remains capable of working with a pleasant tone in the face of the worst disasters and annoyances (hard drives crashing, a barrage of phone calls,

not enough time to work, the director is never satisfied, everyone hates your music, etc.).

7. Very sure *your* vision of a score is the right one, even after your score has been replaced.

Do not be discouraged by criticism, for it may come from someone who cannot see your true abilities. I wasted valuable time finding out that I was going to be a musician. In my senior year of high school I went to the pre-eminent musician in our area, a former trumpet player with the band *Fred Waring & His Pennsylvanians*, who was head of the local college music school. My father took me for a professional evaluation of my musical ability. The professor put a page of piano music in front of me to sight-read, but that was not one of my strengths, and I must have played it poorly. From this short evaluation he concluded that I should go into engineering instead of music, much to my father's delight. Later, because I still wanted to be a musician, I quit engineering school and got a masters' degree in music theory. The moral to this story is to never take criticism too much to heart. Pursue what you love to do, and enjoy the process of becoming what you want to be.

The ability to compose is just a part of what it takes to succeed as a film score composer. Chances are it has at least as much to do with some very important non-musical factors as well, like personality, perseverance, sensitivity to criticism, the town you live in, etc. And when the opportunity arrives, do not hesitate to get help, if need be, to handle the sudden rush of work. Let's imagine the following scenario:

Your networking has paid off big time, and you get a call to write an original feature film score with a big orchestra; the film is of epic proportions and the studio is willing to pay for a comparable orchestra. You suddenly realize you have never orchestrated for this many instruments before and never had to write this much music in such a short time. What to do? The first thing is to get an experienced orchestrator and music editor who have done this before. They can save you time, give you clues as how to maximize your re-use of material, help you decide on the style of music and how it is reflected in the band you hire, and help you choose a contractor and copyist. You can give the orchestrator Standard MIDI Files from your sequencer and audio dubs of your synth mockups, along with a video copy of a rough cut of the film, and he can begin to work. You'll be surprised how fast the orchestrator can work if you do *not* make an attempt to orchestrate everything yourself. If you do orchestrate, he will have to familiarize himself with every note of yours before completing his orchestration, which can take valuable time better spent elsewhere.

THE ORCHESTRATOR

In the earliest days of film scoring, composers were more often classically trained (e.g., Bernard Herrmann, Erich Korngold, Aaron Copland) and quite capable of orchestrating their own scores. As the need for speed increased, a dedicated orchestrator was added to the process. Today, most film composers use orchestrators, at least for their larger scores, not only to save time but to handle many other tasks as well.

Film composers today are more familiar with computer sequencing than classical orchestration techniques, and understandably so as the sound often comes first and the score later, if at all. (For smaller projects, a synthesized film score might not even see the paper stage but could remain in electronic from start to finish). The perfect liaison between such computer-based composers and the live orchestra is the orchestrator, who translates the composer's MIDI mockups into an orchestral score playable by live musicians. (See Chapter Three, Mr. Mockup).

If composers come in many varieties, then orchestrators complement this diversity by being flexible, familiar with a wide variety of musical styles, and capable of assisting the composer in many ways. For example, as an orchestrator, I have been asked to create film cues from the following:

1. Humming, grunting, whistling, and/or the stamping of feet.

2. A single-word description of a scene—"chaos"—for 30 seconds.

3. Four bars of melody and a request to "fill out" the music for a four-minute, full-orchestra cue.

4. A four-voice hymn texture to be made into a thrashing, swirling, and bombastic Star Wars-type action cue.

5. "Do something like Bartok's 'Music for Strings Percussion & Celeste'" for three minutes.

6. "Make a new cue from the previous one, but maybe more like ..."

7. A MIDI file to be "filled out" (added to) as a sequence, e-mailed back to the composer for additions without it ever being put on paper—"electronic orchestration."

8. A piano demo, which I first transcribe, then arrange.

9. A two- to three-line sketch with dramatic words of instruction.

I have found the best way for a composer to communicate musical intent to the orchestrator is the "two- to three-line sketch" (method #9), along with a video of the entire film and a dub of the MIDI sequenced audio as a guide to any questions that may arise. With these in hand, the orchestrator can work in a quick and unencumbered way toward an orchestrally conceived cue. Again, it is worth reiterating that the more a composer orchestrates, the slower the orchestrator will work, because every note requires a decision as to whether the composer really meant it or whether it should be changed, and that takes time. Experienced orchestrators can work from any sources they are given. Even if a composer gives them nothing at all, they can come up with something. Once, for a recording session, I was asked if I could have an arrangement of a Billy Joel tune for the next session two hours later. Of course I said, "No problem." So I picked up the sheet music of the tune, used the piano reduction as a guide, and wrote directly to pencil parts for each instrument of a nine-piece band, skipping the creation of the usual score because there was no time to get a copyist.

While an orchestrator must be able to work quickly, he must also have endurance. The pace may become very grueling in the final days before a recording begins. The composer may send new cues every couple of hours if he has gotten a group of them approved by the director. This, combined with the fact that composers tend to be nocturnal, puts a real crunch on the orchestrator and the copyist, and they both may need to hire extra help at this stage to meet the deadline.

In addition to speed and endurance, an orchestrator needs a sixth sense for identifying those sounds that are particularly irritating to the composer. You can only know these kinds of things after working with a composer several times, and for that reason, the first time around, the orchestrator may "step on some ears." I remember one composer who dreaded the sound of an oboe while there was dialog; another was aghast at the addition of a third to an open fifth sonority; another was displeased by my having a string run up to a climactic high note (I think he was the same one who loathed anything remotely resembling the sound of John Williams). After hearing an orchestration I did for him, Elliot Goldenthal said to me, "Sounds like Elgar." Always looking for compliments, I said, "Thanks," but probably should have asked whether he liked Elgar (Sir Edward Elgar, English composer, 1857-1934).

In turn, I can tell you something that irritates an orchestrator. Upon seeing computer printouts of the composer's MIDI files, some people will comment, "I guess there's not much left for you to do—it looks like it's all there." Printed music has an uncanny way of looking complete, simply because it looks so neat. However, neatness does not an orchestration make.

Because so many composers today create their scores in MIDI sequences, the orchestrator has to be able to fix them when necessary, clean them up, or align the downbeats for composers who simply use the computer as a fancy recording machine with the click off. Obviously, this slows down the orchestration process considerably and might require yet another person to align and clean the tracks before the orchestrator can work.

In addition to cleaning up MIDI tracks, an orchestrator usually has to condense many of the parts. It is common for a composer, in the heat of scoring a film, to go back to the beginning of a cue and add new tracks for additional ideas as they come to him, rather than alter an existing track. The end result might be a sequence with thirteen legato string tracks and seven pizzicato string tracks, all of which the orchestrator condenses and distributes appropriately into the customary five-line string score. In addition to strings, it is often the percussion section which has too many MIDI tracks for the live players to cover (once I had seventeen tracks for six players), so the orchestrator rewrites the percussion to best accommodate the number of live percussionists on the session. This is an important time-saver that will facilitate the recording of the percussion (See Chapter Nine, Percussion Parts). The occurrence of more lines in the MIDI sequence than players available in the orchestra is one of the main reasons why MIDI *files cannot simply be printed and played by live players* (See Chapter Three, Mr. Mockup).

There are times when a composer chooses not to write certain cues and the orchestrator can be called on to write these cues with some verbal instruction as to style, such as, "For cue 3M7 take the main title and do it in a West Coast jazz style," or "take cue 4M9 and give it a romantic twist instead of the intrigue feel." This can be fun for the orchestrator, and it can give the composer valuable time to do other things. Once a composer gave me a small melodic fragment and said, "Add, add, add—take material from the end and put it in the front to make it organic." The same composer also gave me one of the most interesting instructions I ever had when he simply said to take a certain tune and think, "1934, Vienna, very moody."

Though orchestrators never know what's coming at them from one cue to the next, they'd probably be disappointed if it were otherwise.

THE CONDUCTOR

Often a composer will conduct his own scores, and after each cue is recorded to his satisfaction, he visits the booth to hear a playback with video and get comments from the director. Sometimes the orchestrator may conduct, leaving the composer in the booth with the director. This is an especially good setup if the director is unfamiliar with the recording medium in general or needs a lot of support from the composer. Much less often, a professional conductor will be hired for the sessions. This leaves the composer free to be with the director and concentrate on how the score is working with the film, and the orchestrator can be either orchestrating new cues or helping tweak the one being played at the moment, or both.

In my experience, composers and orchestrators are usually capable conductors, familiar with the recording session routine and the intent of the music. They know the music at hand very well, and if the score uses a click track (which it often does since it is usually created in a sequencer program), they realize that presenting an artistic beat pattern is not as important as communicating the feel or attitude of the score. Studio musicians are accustomed to conductors of all kinds, good and bad, and they adjust to each situation. As for the players, they probably prefer the composer as conductor, regardless of his conducting skill, because they are getting instruction directly from their employer, and the more personal contact with him the better for future work.

THE MUSICIANS

These people are usually so musical, versatile, and ready for anything that we take them for granted. Trumpet players with high-range endurance that is not supposed to exist, woodwind players who can play phrases so long and beautiful you'd think they'd turn blue, pianists who can sight-read huge piles of notes perfectly, eight bassists who can pizzicato as one, French horn players with superhuman agility on a less-than-agile instrument, trombonists who play in the trumpet range—they all never cease to amaze me. (These things aren't listed in your orchestration books). And, in addition to playing anything that is written, they can also play things that are not, like, "Repeat bar 7 up an octave, segue to bar 14 for three bars, then go to bar 1 but only play every other note of it, and molto legato please."

The more you work with players the more you begin to realize their particular strengths. You may discover a legit flute player who can swing, or a timpanist who is also a great drum set player, or a jazz sax player who can also play the bassoon part in the *Marriage of Figaro* overture. The downside of this luxury is that you begin to think this is the norm.

THE DIRECTOR

Film directors are a wide-ranging lot, and sometimes their musical experience can be sketchy. If so, the composer should be patient and careful not to use too many musical terms that may make them feel uneasy. Directors can feel out of their element, now that their film has locked, the actors have left, and the project has moved to the composer's turf. Fortunately there is the synth mockup, a real boon for directors in the whole scoring process because they usually *do* know what music they do *not* want in their film when they hear it.

I knew one director who became very disoriented by the sheer sound of a 70-piece orchestra. Everything sounded too big to him. We proceeded to take out as much of the orchestra as possible *before* he heard it because he said that *after* he heard it with everyone, it was impossible to hear it any other way. My job as orchestrator became making the orchestra sound as small as possible—a very unusual twist on my normal function. Usually I am asked, "We can only afford 20 musicians, can you make it sound like *Star Wars?*"

Another curious experience was when a young second time director, anxious to make his mark for a Disney film, said at an initial meeting with the composer and me that he wanted the music to sound as if "you took all the instruments and threw them down the stairs." We both just calmly said, "Sure, no problem," and went on with our job, not knowing exactly what he meant. He never said any more about it.

Another time, with the same director, there was a loud brass melody that he hated in the synth mockup. The cues with that melody had already been orchestrated and copied, so we left them alone, and when the real orchestra played it, the loud live brass sounded fine to him. It must have been the quality of the synth sounds that made him dislike the melody in the first place. More to the point, this illustrates the overwhelming effect the orchestral sound can have on even the most skeptical listener and it brings up a strange twist on Murphy's law: Sometimes, things you think will go wrong simply go away. The trick is to know ahead of time which will be forgotten and which will not.

Directors have certain instruments they dislike, and it's your job as the orchestrator to figure out which ones they are and be ready to fix them, quickly, at the session. One director objected to any kind of harp, but the harpist was already hired, so I gave her a part to play, just nothing very prominent.

We all usually try our best to please the director, but sometimes you must be careful of trying too hard. On one session, after a long series of changes to a cue trying to please a director, when all ideas left us, we returned to the original form of the cue, to which the director replied, "Yes, that's good." We had come full circle, realizing too late that whatever caused his original discomfort was a very small thing that should not have wasted so much time. Once, a composer kept changing a cue in an effort to get an enthusiastic approval from director Robert De Niro. An hour later, a very patient Mr. De Niro said, "I liked the first one." Very often, any complaint a director may have is caused by a small musical element that can be fixed by such maneuvers as removing the eighth-note motion in the violas, or by taking out the trumpets in a certain place. Rarely is the change a difficult one to actually make; it's finding out what the change should be that is tricky. Remember, if your synth mockups were approved earlier, any fix at the recording session should not be that big. Look for small fixes first.

If there is a musical "temp" track, it pays to know beforehand what parts of it the director is "married to" and what parts are least important. The term refers to "temporary" music that the music editor has laid in the video so the film can be shown to preview audiences before the original score is complete. If the director refers you to the temp track and asks, "Why doesn't your score sound like that?" your job is to convince him that your score is *better* than the temp. Unfortunately, "temp love" is sometimes so strong that even the biggest composers cannot get around it. It is a fact that pieces of temp tracks have actually displaced scores by the biggest name composers because they would not agree to do a score like the temp track. Some composers, such as Philip Glass, will not score a film if there is a temp track involved. All composers would rather not deal with them, sometimes to the point of ignoring them altogether. Even when the directors have used the composer's *own* music as a temp track, it puts the composer in a very tough spot having to do the same thing again, but differently. The only good thing about temp scores is that they can be helpful in showing the composer the kind of music a director might like in his film. Without it, the composer and director could spin their wheels for weeks before coming to common ground.

The director is usually the boss, except when you have a young director and an older, more experienced film editor is really making the decisions for him, or a producer is there to offer guidance. The very worst scenario, which fortunately does not happen often, is when the director and the studio cannot agree on edits so there are two separate versions of the film, and the composer has to somehow run down the middle of the two, hoping to satisfy both camps. Later, in Chapter Seven, Fix It, there is more about pleasing the director by making fixes to the existing music instead of throwing it out.

THE MUSIC EDITOR

One of the most multi-talented and unsung heroes of the entire film scoring process is the music editor. Often a composer in his own right, the music editor understands the composer's point of view and is also familiar with the technical considerations that have to be included in the process, communicating to the scoring engineer (mixer) the most musical way of accomplishing them. Seeing all sides of a three-sided coin, the music editor is a liaison between the director, composer, and mixer.

The music editor begins work early in the film scoring process by attending the spotting sessions with the composer and director to figure out where music should occur in the film and to explore the benefits of doing something one way versus another. He can be especially helpful to a new film composer. One of the music editor's most important jobs early on is to build the temp score for the director to use at previews of the film for small audiences, where they ask for comments from the audience on cards to gauge the general reaction to the film. I have been told that on one film there were 17 different previews, all having somewhat different temp scores. This job alone is staggering when you think of the familiarity a music editor must have with hundreds of soundtracks to be able to find the temp music he needs with the right dramatic shape for each scene.

Traditionally, the music editor assigns cue numbers to all cues and creates spotting and timing notes for the composer, listing all the cues, locating starts and ends of cues in SMPTE timecode (See Chapter Ten, Practice), with brief descriptions of the dramatic function of each cue. These notes show the first overview of the entire musical score, giving the composer a panoramic look at what has to be done. For a lengthy mini-series project, I remember seeing file cards covering an entire wall to show the whole project at a glance, and we would take the cards off the wall as cues were completed. Eventually a composer may create his own cue list showing which ones employ which themes, and how the cues will be distributed among the various size bands that may be used. It is not unusual for a score to use two or three different-size orchestras—small, medium, and large—depending on the cue.

At the recording session, if the composer is not generating a click track from a sequencer, the music editor will have made clicks for each cue that needs them. The music editor usually starts the click source for the conductor, or if the band is not playing to click, he has a computer program ready to give the conductor streamers if needed. In addition, a music editor keeps track of which cues are finished and which have to be recorded, keeping an eye on how much time remains. If a cue has to be moved to accommodate a new edit or if a new click has to be found, the editor is there. Sometimes the director will feel an urge to move a climax point either forward or backward, and the editor can quickly figure out a musical solution by adding or subtracting beats, telling the orchestrator and conductor what to change.

With the advent of Pro Tools software (and the less popular but more sophisticated Sonic Solutions), music editing has moved to a new level. The editor's job can now include post-recording fixes where he manipulates the score to fit a scene more closely, stretching or shrinking where necessary. Some composers record a few very long cues first and then, with the help of their music editor, cut, paste, and rework sections of a big cue to make smaller ones. Budget permitting, they can re-record the new smaller cues. Also, the music editor is responsible for laying-in any pre-existing pop tunes purchased by the studio for inclusion in the film.

After the recording sessions are over, the music editor must attend the necessary, final film re-recording session where dialog, effects, and music are brought together and balanced for the final print. Here the editor must be the "protector of the score," in that the music inevitably gets reduced in volume or moved around if left to its own defenses. It is unequivocally the most laborious part of filmmaking, the one job that evens out the balance for all the fun things. Sidney Lumet said in his book *Making Movies,* "To make up for the joy of seeing Sophia Loren every morning, God punishes the director with the mix." Ten minutes of film can take an entire day to mix, so there is a good week or two of playing small sections of the film over and over and over for setting the relative levels of each sound.

THE MIXER

Formerly called the "recording engineer," this person is in charge of the mixing console and everything that goes in or out of it. He usually has an assistant or two to do all manner of things in the studio involving the setup of equipment, monitoring the headset cue system, keeping track of all mics, baffles, music stands—even the temperature of the room.

Most composers are faithful to their mixers and use the same one indefinitely, and for good reason. It takes time for the mixer to become familiar with a composer's preferences for sound, mics, pacing, mixing technique, and so on. A mixer familiar with a composer's style can begin mixing on his own time before the composer is finished writing and recording the score, which gives the composer more time for other things.

Mixers who are also musicians definitely have an edge. If the conductor does not have much experience and has trouble waving his arms and listening at the same time, the mixer can point out places where the band is out of tune, not rhythmically together, or where there was room noise. If a mixer is an experienced musician, he can tell when the band is not living up to its potential. Mixers who are very attentive to the sound quality might say, "Trumpets, would you please tilt your horns up above the music stand at bar 27," to get a brighter sound. A good mixer calls the conductor's attention to anything that might sound like a problem he heard in the booth but was maybe inaudible in the conductor's headphones.

No one is more experienced at hearing separate parts of an orchestral sound than the mixer. Good ones can instantly hear if the strings and woodwinds are articulating their phrases together or if the oboe was playing in the tutti section, or if the bass drum and bass should have the same figure. It is no fun to be listening to the mix after the band has left and realize that someone made a mistake or that a detail of phrasing was not coordinated. The ears of the mixer are so helpful. You want the input of a good one. But, if he is prone to give more input than necessary, he can actually become less than helpful. A good mix of "info to gab" is important for a mixer to know.

A mixer who can foresee problems during recording that could arise later at the mix might suggest that the percussion should be overdubbed for control over their sound, or that the brass is wiping out the woodwinds so you should record the brass as an overdub to have control over them as well. Mixers who read scores are an even bigger help because they can do things such as remind the piano and harp they are unison at a certain measure and ask if they can hear each other. From the band list and a short preliminary discussion of the style of the music, the mixer can devise the best seating arrangement of the players to allow for an effective bleeding of sound from one group to another, or which instruments need to be in a separate room (like bagpipes!). Never wait until the session to tell the mixer of an important instrument change that will affect the setup. It will cost you time—and money—while the change is made. Also, the mixer should be apprised of the order of recording cues so that the right video can be prepped and (for analog overdubs) the right reels of tape are set to go.

Last, but most important, you should know before hiring a mixer whether his experience complements your music. Trying to get a rock and roll mixer to record a symphony orchestra can be an impossible task, so if the recording studio says, "The mixer is included in the price of the studio," do not let it go at that. You need to know what kind of work he has done.

THE CONTRACTOR

Beginning composers who are used to small bands probably are unfamiliar with the job of the contractor. In selecting one, you should ask the busier recording musicians which contractors they have worked for and what was the style of music being played. A good contractor makes every effort to hire the right musicians for the style of music to be played. For example, hiring legit players for music that is supposed to swing can be a disaster. If you find yourself in that situation, don't waste time trying to make it work. Either record without them or let that music wait until another session, when you'll have the right players. Also, it is important to find a "lead" percussionist who can advise you about other percussionists to hire so you will have a section that is cohesive and will "groove" when necessary.

Just as with a mixer, you want a contractor whose experience will enhance your score. Ask which composers they have worked with and find out whether they have booked sessions for your style of score. You might want to let the contractor hear some of the synth mockups to get an idea of the style involved and thereby have a better idea of what players to hire.

Before the contractor can begin hiring musicians, he will need a complete list of what instruments you will need, including all woodwinds, brass, strings, and percussion; which mutes for brass are needed; how many and which timpani; if contrabasses need the "C extensions;" piccolo or E♭ trumpet for high brass; if any ethnic instruments have been added; and so on. Booking a large orchestra takes a number of days to finalize. After the calls go out to the players there is a waiting period before they all respond (especially around holidays), and alternate players have to be contacted when first-call players are not available, so give the contractor enough time to get you a good band. When the band list is finalized and before each session, the contractor should prepare and place on the conductor's podium a list of all the players on that particular session listed by instrument and name, so the conductor can identify them personally when necessary. I try to keep a copy of these for future reference so I can refresh my memory about a certain player from a previous session.

As soon as the contractor knows the number of musicians and hours of recording, they can provide you with a pretty accurate budget, including all the extras such as cartage fees for instruments like harp, performers who get double scale, charges for supplies, etc. Be prepared for a total greater than you might have expected if you are used to non-union gigs because of the extra union charges like health benefits and pension. A wise contractor always estimates a budget a little above the minimum required to cover any extra players or unexpected costs down the line. Try to anticipate any overtime or overdub sessions, and be sure they are reflected in the budget.

To estimate how many hours of recording time you will need, figure that in one three-hour session you can record between seven and ten minutes of score. This includes time for playback before going on to the next cue and the ten-minute break per hour. It is possible to record more than that per session if the music is very simple to play and you eliminate some of the playbacks with video. (Incidentally, if your video is analog tape there can be some time lost at a session waiting for the tape machine to rewind and lock to picture).

Do not hesitate to ask the contractor for anything involving the players before or during the sessions, such as contacting players in advance or sending them parts or requesting info about instruments. Also, in the unlikely event you may have some unruly players disrupting a session by excessive talking or intentional wrong notes, don't let it continue or try to fix it, simply ask the contractor to take care of it. It is his job.

The Music Copyist

Have you ever thought about the fact that the profession which has been solely responsible for giving us the entire classical music literature for the past 400 years or so has recently become extinct? That is the hand music copyist. Musical scribes were our gateway to the past. Computer notation programs have now become so easy to use and are so compatible with the sequencing routine used by most composers that, unless the band is pretty big, copyists are not even called because the parts can be printed easily. Not a happy thought if you have hand-copying friends who for some reason have not made the transition to the new software. But let's look on the bright side. My copyist friend, Emile Charlap, who had never used a computer in his life, at the age of 80 was able to learn how to extract parts from my scores in Sibelius after only a couple of hours, and was amazed at how simple it was.

The days of snail-mailing scores and parts to Europe and hoping they arrived on time, or at all, is a thing of the past. Nowadays, with e-mail, even FedEx and faxing are too slow—we are in a speed-based business like everyone else. Copyists everywhere can come to the aid of their distant friends because of time differentials. They no longer have to be in the same city to join forces. I can remember early morning panics where all the music prep people would gather at the copying office at 6 a.m. to get ready for a 10 a.m. session. Not anymore. I've worked on projects where the composer was in London, the director in California, the orchestrator in New York, and the copyist in Australia. It is very efficient but admittedly not nearly as much fun as the old way, with all the jokes, stories, and general camaraderie.

Because it is possible for non-musicians to learn the part extraction process, you must be careful that your electronic copyist is aware of the conventions of music preparation that the players expect to see on their parts. There is generally more space on parts for a recording session because it makes sight-reading easier. There is generous spacing between notes, fewer bars per stave than normal, bar numbers below each measure, and page turns carefully thought out. These and other conventions must be recognized or you will pay for it in time lost correcting parts at the session.

It is usually the composer or orchestrator who chooses the copyist he wants to use. In choosing a copyist, it is important to have someone who is aware of the usual time crunch as the project approaches the recording dates, and who accepts it as a normal part of the job. The copyist always gets the brunt of everyone else's procrastination because he comes last in the score preparation process and usually gets very little time to do his work. He should have a staff he can call into action when needed so that there is no wasted time when scores are ready. It is now common for the copyist to be working *in* the studio as the first session begins so new scores are being copied even after recording begins.

Consider the copyist's schedule when possible and don't give him 25 scores on Friday and expect all cues to be ready for the 10 a.m. start on Monday. You can only record one cue at a time, and if you demand everything to be on the stand at the start, it will only cost you more in overtime and extra fees he will charge to get it all done. Avoid this by telling him which cues you would like to start with.

In addition to preparing parts, the copyist can assist at the recording session in many ways. He will have a librarian who has proofed the parts, organized them into part books for each instrument and has them on all the players' music stands ready for the downbeat. The librarian can also be prepared to answer any questions the players may have about wrong notes.

The copyist should keep an on-going percussion list of what instruments are needed as he works on each score and should give it to the contractor or the lead percussionist days in advance so all the instruments are on hand. This information will show up also on a chart called the "orchestra breakdown," which the copyist prepares showing cues that are complete (updated per session), the title and number of the cue, length in bars, and, most importantly, which instruments are playing on each cue, represented by check marks in columns. This can help in deciding which cues to play at which session—e.g., if the brass are only coming to the morning session, you want to be sure that no brass cues are forgotten.

Occasionally at a session the orchestrator may choose to try a different instrument for a certain part (e.g., having an oboe play what originally was a solo muted trumpet). Because there is a difference in the instruments' transpositions, a new part can be created easily at the session by having the copyist print a new oboe part with the trumpet music included in his key. Before computers, this could take much longer. The copyist's presence in the studio is also helpful when, for example, an ethnic instrument shows up and the part is not written in the most convenient key. A quick change of transposition and the copyist can print a more suitable part.

Many years ago, when I was music librarian for a film recording session, the copyist/contractor Emile Charlap reminded me to bring manuscript paper and pencils in case we had to make a fix on the spot. After seeing the huge stack of paper I started to bring, Emile said, "If we need *that* much paper we are in big trouble." True, because in those days, how much could one or two people copy while the band is waiting for a part change? Today, the computer enables the copyist to make many more quick fixes at the recording session.

THE STUDIO EXECUTIVES

Every major feature film scoring session is usually attended by the film producers and heads of music at major studios. They will come by for a day or two, and are most often pleasant, complimentary and supportive. Their project is becoming a reality after a year or two in the works, and everyone shares their relief and anticipation for a successful run. They are no cause for alarm, however their presence is the main reason we ask our friends not to visit the recording session too early on, but wait until things have settled into a routine, which it usually does very quickly.

The most valuable part of meeting these people is to get a small glimpse as to how the higher-ups view the whole film scoring process. They rarely make any big waves this late in the post-production schedule since a deadline is fast approaching. They are there because lots of money is involved, and, like any corporation, they want to have executive oversight. It is unusual for these people to actually have any creative input, but as a composer's reputation grows, so too the support and recognition from the executives.

Once, at a recording session, a producer had to be present in the booth to keep an errant director from straying too far afield, as he was prone to do (like skip off to karate lessons), and so the producer would occasionally say, in an effort to exert some kind of control after each playback, "okay, what are we doing next?" after which he would immediately get back on his cell phone and talk very loudly while we were trying to record, completely oblivious to the process at hand. This is the exception.

The producers give us a reality check. They remind us that the project at hand is first a business proposition, and second a creative playground. And despite this fact, a major pop culture media force, like a film studio, with enough money to finance extremely expensive films can, in the end, be the benefactor of what often turns out to be a very exciting and worthwhile endeavor.

Getting started

*T*he most common question I get from film scoring students is undoubtedly, "How do I get started working in the film business?" Understandably, after you have done all the preparation possible (taking classes, studying scores, writing as much as you can for fellow student projects, honing your abilities as composer, orchestrator, performer, recording engineer, etc.), you eventually feel you are ready to move on to the next level and start getting paid for your talent and dedication.

I tried to prepare myself for as many different situations as I could before coming to New York. Performing, composing, arranging, and teaching were all areas I enjoyed, so I did them as best I could and tried to be ready for any opportunities I could find.

When I arrived in the late 1970s, Emile Charlap was (and still is at age 85) a legend in the New York recording scene. He has worked with nearly anyone you can name as a contractor and/or copyist, and for many years had an office on 48th Street with several rooms where arrangers could write with a piano and some A/V equipment. It was also a great place to meet other musicians. Some very famous people would pass through, like Dizzy Gillespie, Billy Joel, Phil Ramone, Arif Mardin, Ralph Burns, Gil Evans, Johnny Mandel, etc. and many not-so-famous, but very talented people. A friend from school (trombonist Jim Pugh) introduced me to Emile. I was anxious to do anything; just to work in the Big Apple was a dream I could not wait to realize. Bill Waranoff, an arranger working with Emile, said there were some lead sheets in the back room that no one wanted to transcribe. Would I be interested? I jumped at the chance—at last, a real job in the big city! My transition to the film business came when the film composer, Michael Small, asked Emile for someone to arrange a few source cues for a film, and since I happened to be around, Emile sent Michael to me. When asked if I had ever written for marching band, I replied, "Are you kidding?" Actually, I had not, but I knew, since Michael had a tape of the sound he wanted, there would be no problem. Thanks to Emile, I began to orchestrate for Michael on a number of films and commercials, and that gave me my first credits to pass around with a demo reel.

My progress toward anything you could call a financially solvent music career was slow in coming. I was patient and enjoyed the variety of each project, all the while still doing lead sheets for Emile and working as librarian for large orchestra sessions where I would hand out the music and fix any wrong notes as they came up. But, the greatest advantage was that the librarian and orchestration jobs gave me a front row seat to the live orchestral sound, which I had never experienced before, as I was a pianist who played mostly with small bands. And, like most orchestration students, I had taken classes but never heard a note of what I wrote; we got teacher comments in red— "too high," or "too low"—and that was about it. So the recording sessions I could attend were like orchestration classes, the difference being that there was no teacher, just fabulous live musicians and scores. At the sessions, each group of instruments would be rehearsed separately, for balance, and I could watch the scores go by and glean a wealth of first-hand experience I could not have gotten any other way. I walked through the orchestra as it was playing to hear all the nuances of sound, a rare treat that I still enjoy.

Did I seek out a career as an orchestrator? Not until I started to see how much fun it could be, hearing music I put on paper played by the finest musicians in the world and not having to deal directly with any of the arguments or disagreements in which a film can get entangled.

I now realize that the best thing I ever did was to put myself in daily contact with people who were in a business that looked exciting and fun. I was in New York City because that was the hub of the music world for an East Coast-type like myself. I wanted to be near the action so that if a break came, I could jump in. At that time, being in the right city was important. If you could find someone like Emile Charlap with a room where musicians hang out, that would be a terrific place to start.

MEETING PEOPLE IN THE BUSINESS

You should meet not only directors for whom you want to compose, but anyone in the business who could help you make contacts, such as other composers, orchestrators, directors, actors, music editors. You could attend conferences sponsored by The Film Music Society, seminars sponsored by Film Music Network, or film festivals of new works by young filmmakers. You could take a few classes at a school that offers film scoring (e.g., New York University, USC, UCLA, Berklee College of Music) or attend their summer workshops (such as the NYU summer film scoring workshop). Sometimes teachers may know of music jobs that students can apply for, as they are usually found by word of mouth. Your best contacts could be young directors you meet at school who will go on to bigger and better things. Keep lists of your contacts and try to stay in touch with them. A good source of contacts could be the bulletin boards of a drama or film school, where there might be notices of projects that need composers.

Attending a recording session or a film shoot could be very instructive, but don't expect to hand out a lot of business cards. The people you observe are working and it is not the best time to be selling yourself. However, they might have you join them for a lunch break where the talk gets more informal and maybe the conversation will get to you and what you do; that could be helpful. But generally, don't get in the way or try to be too clever, insightful, or entertaining because all of your good intentions could be taken as simply irritating and hurt more than help. Be open and sincere but low-key, and if you are asked to help out with anything, gladly do it without discussing credit or payment. There is plenty of time for that later. First you need to make friends in the business.

And never go to the first recording session of a series, but let them get into a routine and past any problems that have to be worked out. The second or third sessions are more relaxed, and you will feel much more welcome. Try sitting in the booth for a while, but don't overstay your welcome. One three-hour session should be okay but back-to-back sessions might be a bit much. Also try to spend a little time in the studio with the musicians to hear the difference in sound, but keep your talk to a minimum unless they are on a break. Remember, too, when talking in the presence of mics, that what you are saying might be heard in the booth, and any criticism should be kept for another place.

Success Stories

• I know of a composer who, in a time of need, did some window washing for his brother-in-law (NYC style, on a scaffold that went up and down the side of a building). As he was working, a casting director inside an apartment saw him and asked for his card, later casting him in a soap opera. When they found out he played guitar, they worked that into the show as well, and he even got to compose some music for a later show.

• A composer was at a performance of a play and during intermission began talking with the person next to him, who turned out to be an actor who was in rehearsal for a film that needed a composer. The composer got the contact info and eventually was hired to write the score.

• A violist came to a music contractor's office just to introduce herself. As she was leaving, the contractor got a call for a large string section and he needed violists. He quickly yelled, "Is that girl still here?" The violist he had just met was still waiting at the elevator (good thing it was a slow one), and she got the first of many jobs as a recording musician.

• A first-time composer contacted a film school about meeting with any director who might need a film composer. The composer arrived, met the chosen young director and eventually did his first score with him. What he realized only later was that he had mistakenly taken another composer's interview and through this error went on to do many films with the late director Alan Pakula.

Opportunities can come from literally anywhere. Maybe you could try a slightly different approach than you've tried before. If you have been looking for composing work, try arranging or performing. Or, try an area of music you have *no* experience in. Remember that the famous director Sidney Lumet, on more than one occasion, hired a composer precisely because he had *not* previously scored a film (most notably Quincy Jones for the film *The Pawnbroker*).

NETWORKING ON THE NET

One nice thing about the Internet is the response rate you can get from e-mail. With snail mail, the going rate of replies of any kind is supposedly around 3%. Several years ago I wondered if it would be possible to increase my client base through an Internet blitz campaign, so I did a test. I e-mailed all the film composers for whom I could find addresses and inquired if they had an orchestrator; I received a response of more than 30%. The bad news was that little valuable work ever came from this, because the composers I contacted either had no use for an orchestrator if their work was with small bands and synths, or, they already had someone. The number of cold contacts you can make is enormous, but whether they are the right ones is the question.

I had a Web page for a while that yielded mostly inquiries from beginning film score composers, along with a few professional composers seeking orchestrations. While the idea of the Internet seems appealing, my feeling after testing it is that jobs such as film scoring depend on word-of-mouth, and meeting people personally is a more fruitful approach. True, sometimes one contact is all you need, if it is the right one. Who knows? You might meet up with your own "Merchant and Ivory," two successful filmmakers who have used the same composer, Richard Robbins, for nearly all their films.

PROMOTIONAL DEMOS

Before you get your hopes up too high, there is something you should know about demos in general: *Very few people listen to them.* As any scriptwriter will tell you, he probably gets work not from people actually reading his scripts, but through the efforts of someone selling the "idea" of his script, because the actual script will be changed a hundred times before shooting. If, as one Hollywood biographer has noted, no one in Hollywood reads scripts, I would also venture a guess that no one listens to music demos, either. But, let's look on the bright side and prepare for the best; keep in mind some of the following tips for getting a favorable response.

1. Limit the number of pieces to four or five. When there are too many cuts listeners tend to avoid listening, based on a feeling of "I should hear it all or nothing." Since they don't have an hour to listen, they hear nothing.

2. Keep all pieces in the same genre. Do not try to include every style you've ever written in, but rather, concentrate on tracks that make people say, without a doubt, "That sounds like film music." This is not the place for a student recital performance of your trumpet sonata. Titles of obscure

student films will mean nothing to most people; so do not hesitate to simply label them "Track 1, Track 2, etc. with a heading of "Original Film Music." They know you're not John Williams, yet.

3. Include the duration of each track on the label so the listener will know his time commitment. It is very important to limit the duration of each track to one minute or less for the first demo. If they request more, then you might give them longer tracks.

4. No audiocassettes; those days are gone.

5. No long spaces between tracks (no more than three to four seconds).

6. Equalize the tracks so they are consistent in sound quality. A good engineer can help you balance them so there is no great change from track to track.

7. Avoid choosing tracks that use cliché synth presets or electronic effects. If you must use synth tracks, choose only those that reflect the best sounds you have, not the "cheesier" side of your setup.

8. Avoid tracks with any obvious compromises, such as room noise, out-of-tune instruments, or obviously bad performances. Also avoid sloppy-looking artwork or cover letters.

9. Offer to provide more demo material if they wish, and of course include all of your contact info.

These things will give your demo a professional quality but will not include too much material or too many choices for the busy prospective listener to process quickly. His time for you is limited, so you want your CD to look interesting, be attractively made (not gaudy or overly showy), and *short*. If you really want to show different talents (country western songwriter, techno freak, etc.), make separate CDs for each one limited to four one-minute tracks, clearly labeling each style. That way, the listener can choose what he prefers to hear.

Include a credit list or film music resume that is *only* about your film work (or closely related). I can't imagine anyone in the film business caring which high school you went to or that you won a debate award senior year. Conventional resume writing programs or resume writing services that are not familiar with musicians or the film business are generally not too helpful. In fact, they can look very amateurish because they encourage you to include lots of things that are of no interest to people in such a specialized field as filmmaking.

One traditional resume item is very important: *references.* If you can, mention people that your recipient will know and can easily ask about you. Or, if they don't know them, at least include names they might recognize. This is called *name-dropping,* an art form in Hollywood. It is something everyone does, yet everyone criticizes others for doing. The most desirable technique is to do it just enough to impress people, but not enough to lose the job.

WHAT TO DO WITH YOUR DEMO

One of the best sources I've found for locating films in production that might need original music is one of the most popular trade magazines, *The Hollywood Reporter.* There is a daily version and a weekly one. Look for the weekly issue that includes small two-inch listings of films currently in production (not all of the issues you might see on the magazine rack have it). Once or twice a year, they even devote the entire magazine to film music, and these are especially interesting ones, including interviews with film composers and lists of film composers and their agents, as well. There is also a Web site where you can get this info online for a monthly fee of about $20.00 (**www.hollywood reporter.com**). Their listings include the names of all cast and crew hired so far, such as the director, screenwriter, producer, and actors, along with the shooting start date, shooting locations, name and address of the film company, and often a telephone, fax number, or e-mail address.

You could start by looking for small independent companies in or near your city. It is usually the director who chooses the composer, so try to contact him first. It is not likely that the director of the latest Mel Gibson film will be interested in talking to you, since big-budgets films get their composers through agents or recommendations of the director. Try for smaller films with a crew and cast larger than a single person (sometimes the listing is obviously a one-man show, and your rewards there might not be commensurate with the work you will have to do). While personal meetings are always better than phone calls, faxes, or e-mails, before dropping in on any prospective clients, you should call to see:

1. If they are accepting composer "submissions" for original film music.

2. Which format they prefer: CD, DVD, VHS or MP3. Frequently just audio CDs are preferred, but having a few video clips ready can't hurt.

3. If you can deliver your demo in person and talk with someone like a director or producer. They will probably tell you to mail it, but do everything you can to make a personal visit. "No problem, I'm going to be in your area anyway." You might run into the director.

You can expect:

1. To meet a wide variety of people (to say the least).

2. To be ignored (treated like the pizza delivery boy).

3. To have some directors look at your demo as music in its final form, which they are expected to accept or reject as is. You must inform them that writing an original film score is supposed to be a living, collaborative process in which you can change things they might not like.

4. That if you offer to compose a single cue for their unfinished film "on spec," it's not really showing what a film composer can do in creating relationships between characters and scenes. Also, if you see only one cue from the film, chances are your one guess for the appropriate music for this cue will not be what the director has in mind. You must realize that by doing this you are putting yourself at a big disadvantage. Wait until there is a rough cut of the whole film.

AGENTS

Names of film score composers' agents are included with a long list of composers in the special film issue of the *Hollywood Reporter*. (If that issue isn't due out for several months, you might be able to get a back issue directly from its New York or Los Angeles offices or through the Web site, **www. hollywoodreporter.com**). There is also another Web site, **www. soundtrack.net/representation,** that has a very extensive list of agents. In both cases, be sure to check that the information is current.

Agents will generally not be interested in you until you have scored a feature or two that they can use for promotion. Even if you have a feature to promote, they spend most of their time on their highest profile clients, not their newer ones. So, if you do land an agent, you still can't sit back and wait for the jobs to come pouring in. You will have to get the work yourself, and then give the agent his usual percentage for negotiating a contract for you. One way of getting started with an agent might be to get your own film scoring job for which you need a contract and ask an agent if he will negotiate it for you. It makes you look more like an asset than a liability in their eyes.

Composition 3

*F*ilm composers are given a film and asked to make choices about what music they think will go with it. That's all. Just make some choices and they'll let you know what they think. Michael Small was composing the music for a film Elaine May was directing, and I remember thinking what a great compliment she paid him by simply saying, "Nice choices, Michael."

TRUST YOUR INSTINCTS

We try so hard to please that sometimes we forget to trust our instincts. We think of who will be listening, what composer they might have preferred to have, and so on. Trust your first impressions. Keep the pencil moving (or nowadays the sequencer rolling) and do what you know for sure first, and don't look back or get caught up in a tangle of self-doubt. No matter the musical training, when it comes to film music, we are all on a level playing field, veteran and novice alike. I know of a film where a young composer was called in to compose five new cues to complete a film score by the legendary John Barry. I don't know why, but whatever the reason, the two composers were considered by the studio to be on par.

If you have twelve days to write twelve cues, force yourself to move on to the second one on day two. If you get stuck doing eight versions of cue one, not only will your musical ideas become exhausted, but also you will put yourself in a very bad psychological state for completing the other cues. When you have finished the twelve cues on schedule or before, you might have ideas for changing the first cue, and if there is time, go back and rework it. Your main focus should be to produce something: grist for the mill, something to take to your meeting with the director to begin a dialog of what course the score will take. There is no one perfect way to write any cue, and nothing is really ever finished until the very last moment, so accept the element of change from day one through the last note of the last recording session, because there will be many changes. Welcome the fluidity of your ideas and be content that, out of several approaches that may come to mind, you have chosen one that you like. You can always go back later to make changes.

LISTEN TO THE SILENCE

You are sent a rough cut of a film you are about to score. Anxious to start, you watch the film with no temp track. If a temp track is there, turn it off until your first impressions have surfaced. You watch it again, because the first time through, you have no ideas. You know the director's concept for music, but you want to develop your own feelings. You have spotting notes from the music editor, and you talked about where the director would like to have music, but you don't agree completely. That's okay. If you see a place where you feel music would work, put it in, and likewise, be prepared to give your case for sections where you think the film should have none. That shows you are not simply assuming an employee posture and that you care as much as the director about creating the best score.

Some composers will watch a film 20 times before something starts to click—ideas start to surface from some unknown place, rhythms, both audible and those produced by visual cuts, start suggesting a melodic or rhythmic pattern from which your first themes will develop. If it is a period film, you might want to steep yourself in music from that time and trust that having done that, your ideas will flow in a similar direction but with your own flavor.

Watch the film intently and take your time in developing the basic themes (usually four or five or so). They must be capable of working in many situations with varied treatments, so they need to be versatile and pregnant with possibilities. Also, you'll be thinking of the consistency of sound throughout, in terms of harmonic language, orchestration, rhythmic impetus, etc.; almost every musical parameter will subconsciously be circulating in your thoughts.

THEMES

Some composers approach a film by simply writing some music reflecting their impressions of the film—not literally to picture, but just general moods and feelings they get after watching it. From these impressions themes can begin to emerge that may be used for particular characters, as in the classic Max Steiner "leitmotif" approach (where characters or places would have themes associated with them). Other composers see the score as creating a more general mood or backdrop against which the film takes place, feeling that film audiences today are sophisticated enough that they don't need to have "Jack's theme" played whenever Jack is in front of them, but rather play what Jack is "feeling." Or the music could play a cross-referencing of feelings that might only be expressed musically, not overtly on the screen.

A director might try conveying to the composer his take on what a theme should be by describing it in words such as "loneliness, sadness, heroism," or simply by saying that the music should be neutral with no feeling at all (certainly the most difficult kind of music to write). The composer then does what he thinks the director wants, not necessarily what he says he wants, because the director may not know how to describe it. He may use the word "pop" to describe a style of music that may actually be more like reggae. His use of the word "medieval" may refer to music that is more like a Baroque gigue from the 18th century. So beware of what words the director is using and consider the possibility that he meant something else. In this regard, the sequencer is a great tool for coming to common ground with the director.

HARMONIC LANGUAGE

Some composers have a default harmonic vocabulary that serves them well on every film they do, while others alter their harmonic settings from film to film. Listen to some horror films with a score by Marco Beltrami or Christopher Young and compare their harmonic language to that of Rachel Portman. I encourage students to think about their default harmonic language, then to venture into the unfamiliar territory of another style. I have seen some composer/pianists become a prisoner of their default pianistic style that refers back to their left-hand chordal formations from their pop tune composing days. Once they realize this, they can make an effort to develop more options, such as composing away from a keyboard, or sitting on their left hand.

Occasionally a director will listen to a cue and remark that it is "too sweet." It may be a result of the orchestration or a harmonic language that is triadic with lots of added 6ths and 9ths, or a melody that sticks close to home with very few leaps. I ask my students to rewrite cues as though I am a director who wants a more dissonant style, but may not know how to put it into words. I may say, "The music doesn't express the character's pain," or, "The music is sweet but the feeling between the two characters is still bitter." Often, student composers will focus on the concluding emotion of a scene and present music which states that emotion throughout the entire cue, failing to mark a point where there is a change from one feeling to another. This gives away the conclusion and defeats the dramatic progression from one feeling to another.

In relation to your own style, consider the two most important elements of dramatic music: tension and motion. They ebb and flow throughout every score in a variety of ways, but exactly how depends on the particular style of the music. Listen to a film, focusing on the element of tension and its release, observe how it is achieved, and do the same with the element of motion. Some very old films had frequent cascades of melodic sweeps up, capped by a tense chord at the peak moment where tension and motion increase at the same time. If you ever see an old silent film done with a contemporary score, it is refreshing to hear new music behind images that we are used to associating with what have become known as traditional Hollywood clichés. Today, tension and motion have found new modes of expression, but regardless of the style, they remain critically important to every score and are the common pivotal elements of both drama and music. For that reason, directors are always concerned about them.

Writer's Block

If you get a case of writer's block, you have to continue work because an unchangeable schedule is upon you. There is no time for waiting until the mood strikes you to write. You will likely have gotten a bunch of CDs from the studio along with phone calls asking you to "make the score like this." For new ideas you can take some of these CDs and put them up against the picture and see what reaction you have. Sometimes taking a 180-degree reversal on your approach to a cue will spark an idea of how to proceed. If you are doing fast action-adventure music that is not working, try a Bach Two-Part Invention or a fast heavy metal track and see what that does. The music editor is another resource you can go to for ideas, since he has already created a temp track for each cue, is familiar with the dramatic intent of each scene, and knows what the director wants. He also has many CDs at his disposal for ideas of how to get on with your work.

Another way to keep moving on a score is a kind of "speed writing." That is, you take a piece of totally blank paper, not even score paper, no lines whatsoever, and simply write, with pencil, rhythms of whatever vague ideas might be flowing through your mind. This can be a liberating experience because it is fast and not sound specific, like a sequencer. You fill in the pitches later, but you can get some idea of what might work texturally for a mood you're trying to capture. Then, you can input your ideas into the sequencer, give them pitch and color and tempo, and see what happens.

An even easier approach is to simply sing into a recorder or, best of all, a digital audio track in your sequencer, any ideas that might come to mind as you view the film. You are making musical comments on the film as it goes by, not only melodies, but any sounds you can make, whistling, tapping, clapping, scraping, etc. This kind of freewheeling approach allows for full concentration on the needs of the film, avoiding any technical or physical concerns associated with performing and recording. We sometimes get so attached to our musical tools, such as a piano or sequencer program, that we lose sight of the fundamental tone of a scene and how to reach our most basic feelings about it.

MUSICAL BAGGAGE

We are all aware of the enormous power of suggestion that music carries with it. All music connotes feelings of some sort and the film composer is often in the position of defining what feeling it is that a director wishes to elicit from a scene. Perhaps without the music there may be little or no feeling, and the music can guide or heighten how the director wishes it to be interpreted. In simple terms, music can reinforce the action on the screen, interpret it, or sometimes, play against what the audience is seeing (e.g., in the Coen Brothers' film *Miller's Crossing*, a lush vocal version of the Irish tune "Danny Boy" plays against a man being chased by killers).

The most difficult music of all to write is that which has *no* musical or emotional connotations—totally neutral. A director may definitely want music for a scene but insists that it must not have any character of its own that would guide or influence the audience in any way. This can be used as a dramatic setup so that the impact of the next scene's music is intensified by the contrast.

The kind of baggage a theme may have can be drastically modulated by the underlying harmonic context. It is common for themes, when they return, to have different harmonic settings, orchestral colors, or degrees of motion surrounding them. It may be a sweet theme, but with a dissonant harmonization and 16th notes in the snare drum it takes on an entirely different character. Of course, there are always exceptions, as when a theme is repeated with exactly the same treatment throughout to emphasize a relentless or un-changing aspect of a character, mood, or place.

HOW MUCH TO WRITE

A typical 40- to 50-minute film score utilizes maybe four to five themes, more or less. This obviously means that themes are going to be repeated in different contexts, which also supports the idea that the less musical info, the better. I know of no feature-length film where the 25 to 30 cues each have a different theme. That is simply contrary to the function of film music. They could use canned music if they merely wanted music that would fit each scene separately, like the temp track. The primary function of the composer is to bring nuances to bear by weaving a quilt of musical ideas in ways that make connections between characters and events. The variation of the score is of prime importance and one of the most difficult concepts to teach about the film scoring process, because we simply never have the time for a student to work on an entire feature in this way. I suppose the closest thing in school to honing this part of the craft is when a student takes one theme and treats it in as many ways as possible—tenderly, violently, sweetly, slow, fast, etc. But you should be prepared to do this kind of thing in the real world, because therein lies your real value as a film composer. Many composers can come up with something that works for the short term, a cue or two, but the real test is whether they can create many variations for several themes that return at interesting moments and in meaningful ways.

If you do happen to write too many themes for a film, don't throw away the extra music. It may prove valuable on another project or as part of an ongoing library of music that you may someday rent to a TV show or small film company as "original canned music" to use as they wish.

With time constraints being what they are in the scoring process, it can be a relief to know that once you have created your basic four or five themes, most everything else will come from them. Also, if there are source cues (meaning cues that are perhaps coming from a live source on screen, i.e., a radio or band) you need not compose these. Give them to the orchestrator or someone who can work on them separately because they have no thematic relation to your score. Also, if you create MIDI files that need to be cleaned up or reoriented so the downbeats occur on beat one, give these to someone else. Your time is too valuable to be doing things someone else can easily do for you.

Once you have recorded some of the larger cues you may consider taking parts of these to make smaller cues with minor variations; this can save a lot of time and still add to the consistency of the overall score. Take a previous cue and copy it for playback with a different scene to see how it works, then make appropriate changes to tempo, harmony, rhythm, etc. The downside of this approach is that copying and pasting can become alluring. I have seen it happen where a composer will "lift" music from one cue to serve another cue, not realizing that he ends up with a few cues in succession that all sound pretty much the same.

Consider recording a few cues in which the orchestra actually watches the video while they are playing a repetitive free figure or improvising on an easily remembered sequence of notes. On the movie *Life*, I had the string players watch monitors to improvise crunching sounds as Eddie Murphy and Martin

Lawrence were running through the woods. The players like these types of challenges, though usually not for an entire score. You have to have enough time to do a few passes to refine your instructions but it is often well worth it. Sounds that are impossible to notate exactly because they are freely improvised can be a refreshing contrast from the usual thematic variation approach.

LESS IS BETTER

One of the most important lessons I learned from working with composer Carter Burwell is that a scene can be carried with far fewer notes than I might have suspected, and that is something I think directors appreciate in a score: simplicity. I constantly ask my students to rethink their scores and eliminate as much as possible, asking themselves what can be taken out without destroying the import of the music. Rarely have I heard a director ask for *more* notes.

A very prolific and accomplished film-scoring student of mine was composing music for a short film by a student filmmaker. The director kept asking for less, less, and even less, to the point he was ready to quit. When the score was complete and I saw the final film, I had to say that I agreed with the director. The composer ended up with a beautifully sparse score that perfectly complemented the light aesthetic of the film. His music was, at first, with full orchestra and it took center stage. Your film score is not a concert. Music used to be more in the forefront of a film, as with Aaron Copland's *Our Town* score and other older examples, but today the role of music has shifted to being more of an integral part of the subconscious background of the film. Some of the best scores are hardly remembered upon leaving the theater, like Howard Shore's *Silence of the Lambs* which is more "felt" than "heard." By writing too much, you may be giving something away in advance, distracting the audience or confusing a relationship by too many themes. Beginning film composers tend to write too many themes with too many notes. It is understandable that directors want as little as possible to interfere with their film. You can make your job easier and your director happier by pulling back on a "notey" concept, staying out of the way as much as possible, then see how often you are asked to add more notes.

If less is more, what about films with no music at all? Studios are not too excited about that approach yet, fortunately for musicians. In fact, studio people get nervous if there is no score. Sidney Lumet has probably directed more films without music than anyone (*Dog Day Afternoon*, *The Hill*, *Network*) or films with ten to fifteen minutes of music (*Serpico* and *Long Day's Journey Into Night*), in which even he had to accede to the studio demands by putting in some music.

SEQUENCER SHORT-COMINGS

Sequencer programs can sometimes lead us down a slippery slope of forgetting to focus on the emotion of a scene, where the tempo should maybe ebb and flow, rubato-like, or even stop completely. Just because the music starts does not mean it has to continue nonstop. It can be refreshing to sometimes take a "swiss cheese" approach around the dialog, meaning simply stop the music when there are words and begin again when there are not, all the while keeping tempo. This is easy to do, and those breaks in sound can be very welcome to the listener's ear, especially when he's trying to hear important dialog.

I remember a film where the music had to build to a big climax, and suddenly a character says just one line of important dialog. What to do? Suddenly pull the music down in the mix to allow the dialog to be heard? Not a good idea. Stop the orchestra entirely for the dialog? Not if you're Mike Nichols. Maybe most of the instruments could stop playing but keep something going, like a high string note or low timp roll, something to sustain the momentum out of the speaking range of the character, then resume when the dialog is finished. That's a good compromise that serves both the dialog and music.

Another warning about sequencer programs: it's easy to forget about dynamics. Because the sequencer does not have visual dynamic markings like a score page, the tendency is to let the volume settings stay in their default position. It is then the orchestrator's job to add dynamics to the score before sending it to the copyist. In the heat of a deadline, they are sometimes left out. A good copyist will catch that and ask the orchestrator to be more specific.

Also, it is possible when composing big scores with lots of brass and percussion to forget about the woodwinds. Because the sequencer playback sounds so good, we think we're done. I get sketches from composers where there are notes written for strings, brass, percussion, and rhythm, with instructions to "give something to the woodwinds." It almost sounds like an act of charity. True, when the brass is big, it takes a special effort to make the winds audible, but that is the great thing about them. They can be swirling around inside a big brassy sound giving interest to a sometimes blocky and dull texture. The woodwind section has so many nuances and unique qualities of sound; they can be used as a separate choir or as a means of shading the orchestra color.

Finally, the MIDI files that sequencers create work far better on the MIDI setup for which they were created than on any other. That is, if you are asked to take your MIDI files to another studio for demonstration, you should be prepared to spend a lot of time preparing the new setup to function exactly like your studio.

If at all possible, you should have the listener (director) come to your studio to hear the mockups. Everything works, no patch routing problems, no sound module differences, and you can make quick changes on the fly that the director might ask for. If you go elsewhere, there can be no end to the disasters that can befall you. Even the best composers can be made to look like bumbling amateurs scrambling to get the same sounds they had at their own studio. Of course, it is possible to dub your MIDI tracks onto audio tracks to convey the sound of your setup, but then you cannot easily make changes as they arise.

To Click or Not to Click

Every sequence created in a computer cannot function without a click of some kind. Even if you don't assign one, it will give you a quarter note at 120. This creates a very strong tendency for composers to succumb to some sort of regular beat in all of their music unless they are aware of the seduction taking place. Our metronomic sequences can lead us into creating scores with an unmusical rigidity if the click of the sequence is used for the conductor and orchestra to follow. It is refreshing to write some cues for *no click* at all (or maybe just click for the conductor) to get away from the rigid feeling. Also, for really quiet cues, it helps the mixer to have no click so he does not to have to worry about click leakage into mics from the headsets.

On the other hand, sequencers can do all manner of ritards or accelerandos to accommodate hits or video sync points, but a word of caution here. When the changes of tempo are too frequent or go from fast to slow only just to catch a hit, it can hurt the feeling of the music. Custom clicks are now commonplace, unlike the days of the click track machine, where they were much harder to create and generally avoided by the clever selection of a click that would accommodate most of the hits. Sections with different clicks would often be recorded separately. I rarely use a click track book or click machine anymore, as the session clicks are usually generated by the sequencer program from the composer's work files.

The advantages of using clicks are self-evident—being able to coordinate very rhythmic cues, or fast tempi with lots of visual hits, along with the fact that cues recorded to click can be intercut to form final takes, so there is a consistency of tempo at the cut points.

If you are a sequencer-based composer who does not like to play to click, you can still use the sequencer to record (with the sound of the click turned off) as you create music locked to the film. But later, someone will have to align all of the downbeats in the sequence so that scores can be created from your MIDI files. This will be costly and time-consuming, but it is your choice. Playing freely with no click is a nice option to use on occasion, although if you do this, the conductor will have to get used to your possibly irregular tempo when he is conducting the orchestra. If there are no critical changes of tempo, it should be okay.

Most sequencer programs give the film composer the ability to insert markers where there are important hits. Then, if you change the tempo, the markers can be locked in real time so you can see how the placement of the hits change position with respect to the beats of each new tempo. This is a very fast way of seeing which tempo best accommodates your video sync points. From there, occasional slight adjustments in the tempi can make your hits more exact, but be careful of drastic changes.

Digitized video in the form of QuickTime files is becoming popular as the chosen medium for digitizing film. They can be viewed on any standard QuickTime player or easily imported into sequencer programs such as Digital Performer or Logic and will be forever locked to the sequence. This eliminates having to sync up the VHS player to the sequencer. The video appears in a neat little corner of the screen, or can be channeled off to a separate monitor.

"Adios" click track machine.

One last pitfall of synth scores you should keep in mind is their ease in switching instrumentation; you can change a synth "band" for each cue, if you want to. Notice that this does not happen in most film scores. While it is possible to change bands for each cue, this can be counterproductive to the focus of a score. By keeping the sound of the orchestra limited to two or three varieties we are diminishing the info expected for the audience to process. There might be large and small orchestras, and a small pop rhythm section. As with themes themselves, the element of orchestration also carries some baggage of connotations that we must keep in mind. A rock band on one cue, orchestra on the next, fife and drum on the third, etc. can become confusing to the listener and distracting. A certain consistency of orchestration helps to unify a score, and taken to its extreme, one of the most unifying techniques a composer has in his arsenal is to associate an important theme with a particular instrument throughout a score. A good example of the effect many different bands can have on a film is *A Bronx Tale*, in which so many different pre-existing pop tunes were used, it created a major distraction.

ORCHESTRATORS

If you have the luxury of an orchestrator, use him. He can save you lots of time. Don't try to orchestrate your MIDI files beyond what is needed for your mockup for the director. Unnecessary MIDI tracks only create more work for the orchestrator, who has to decide what to keep and what to eliminate or change. Three-line sketches are fine, definitely better than 30-line ones. Include verbal comments with your sketch saying where the music is loud or soft, big or small, and any special remarks about the style or rhythmic feel you want. Also, you can ask the orchestrator to construct new cues from ones that have already been orchestrated by giving a few verbal instructions like, "Make cue 3M4 like cue 2M7 but more romantic and lush, much slower but only by 56 seconds."

Your orchestrator can clean up MIDI files if there is time. He can usually conduct also, knowing the score better than an outside conductor might. Give him a complete video of the film even when you think it's not necessary, because there is an osmosis factor that will seep into his work by seeing the film, and that can only be to your benefit. Give him an audio version of your synth mockups (MP3 or CD) that have been approved by the director, along with their relevant MIDI files. This will allow him to work very quickly and keep up with your pace of composing.

At the recording session, you can have the orchestrator change any textures or colors as you go along. You can freely ask him to change tension, motion, balance, dynamics, etc. No need to impress anyone that you have done it all yourself. Everyone is used to seeing orchestrators at the sessions, and their presence can allow you to focus your efforts more importantly on dealing with the director closely.

If the value of an orchestrator is not understood, and you intend to simply print out your MIDI files for the band, perhaps the following scenario will be useful.

"MR. MOCKUP"

Your MIDI score sounds great, the director and studio execs love it, fame and fortune are just around the corner. You're already thinking about what to wear to the Oscars. You print out the parts for the orchestra from your MIDI files, have someone pass them out to the players, wait for that first downbeat and suddenly it doesn't sound so great when you hear the live version. A prominent film composer even told me once when I remarked how glad he must be to get to the point where the live musicians arrive to play his score, he said, "Not really; now I have to make it sound as good as the mockups." So true, especially with the ever-increasing libraries of great synth sounds.

How could the live score not sound as good as your sequences? Can the fault be with the mixer, musicians, contractor, copyist, acoustics of the room, time of day, or room temperature? Or could it possibly be your computer-sequenced orchestrations? Here are some examples of what it might be:

1. Woodwinds and violins are not heard because they are written too low or are covered by the brass. Were the woodwinds an afterthought and just given something to play, doubling the brass?

2. The live strings aren't nearly as lush as your huge-sounding string patches. Budget restrictions limited the number of string players to ten. Use patches for your mockups that are comparable to the live band you will have.

3. That single trumpet part doesn't sound nearly as full as it did at home. You need to add more live brass to emulate the sequenced version.

4. Those tricky rhythms are really sloppy; players are not together like they were in your quantized MIDI.

5. Those patterns alternating between woodwinds and strings are not as tightly together as they should be. Can they hear each other? Are they all wearing their headsets?

6. The budget was big and you were given an orchestra larger than you knew how to handle, so you filled in a lot of doublings just to give players something to do. Now the live band sounds heavy and lumbering.

7. Lots of players are sitting idle and the producer is wondering why they were hired.

8. The live version sounds simpler than you were expecting. Maybe a live orchestra needs more motion distributed inside the texture that is not all just doubling of two or three parts like in the MIDI file.

9. Maybe the mix is a flat acoustical sound, and the solo flute in the low register that you had boosted in your MIDI just isn't coming through above the brass the way you intended.

These are some of the reasons why great MIDI files might not necessarily translate into great orchestrations. Better try using an orchestrator at least until you get your feet wet as to how to get the most sound out of your band. Study what he does with your music—how the brass and strings are filled out, what instrumental registers apply relative to their lowest notes, how inner lines move, how the balance is achieved leading up to those really big moments. You can study this on your own by listening to classical CDs while looking at the scores. Start with simple pieces, like a Haydn or Mozart symphony, and work your way into more complex orchestrations by Ravel, Respighi, or Rimsky-Korsakov.

From MIDI to live orchestra

IDI (Musical Instrument Digital Interface) has had a profound impact on the way people compose and perform music. In essence, it allows an electronic device such as a keyboard to communicate with a computer. Electronic keyboards of some sort are familiar to most kids long before they enter music school, often before first grade. It's the perfect Christmas present for all children, whether they plan on becoming musicians or not. They are cheap and easily produce a huge number of fascinating sounds and rhythms. Some of these keyboards allow the player to record sounds on separate tracks, and there you have the beginning of a MIDI-sequencing studio.

I have even seen, to my surprise, college piano professors choose electronic keyboards for their offices because they sound good enough. Some even have a keyboard touch similar to a grand piano, are easily portable, and can fit into spaces where a grand piano would not. College piano departments, which routinely have the job of teaching piano to every music student in the school, used to have a room full of ten to 20 conventional upright pianos, called the "piano lab." The sound when all were playing was not to be believed! These traditional pianos have now been replaced with electronic keyboards, all with headphone jacks enabling "private" practice; some are connected by a network that allows any number of students to talk with the teacher or play together if they choose.

Nearly every electronic instrument made since the early 1980s has MIDI output jacks for plugging into a computer-MIDI interface. I have even seen *acoustic* pianos and drum practice pads come with a MIDI output jack that can be connected to a computer for use as a controller or trigger. Their instruction manuals usually describe how to expand the built-in sound library by connecting it to external sound modules (or the use of sampled sounds such as those found in GigaStudio). This sometimes begins a never-ending addiction to upgrading with each new sound device as it comes out, and before you know it, you are making so many sounds you begin to lose track of the number you actually have.

Obviously, with so many sounds available, young players get the idea early on that a good way of storing and accessing sounds is with a MIDI sequencing program. After all, you can't play every sound you might want at once (piano, bass, drums, guitar, strings, etc), so entering them one at a time, each sound on a separately recorded track, seems like a good way to go. MIDI sequencing is easy to learn. You can be your own band. You can try all those ideas you wanted to with a live band but without the hassle of trying to schedule a rehearsal for five busy people, or having to find a location where the rehearsal won't bother anyone. MIDI can give you the experience of knowing in advance what your music could sound like with a live band—perhaps not perfectly, but close enough. You have a chance to hear and refine your music so that when you do print the parts for a live band there will be no surprises. MIDI sequencing is truly an amazing way to emulate live musicians, but *do not* assume that the live orchestra you are emulating works exactly the same way that your MIDI one does.

THE MIDI ORCHESTRA

For a few thousand dollars, you can set up a MIDI orchestra on a small desktop with a computer, small MIDI keyboard, and adequate speakers. Your sequencer program (such as Mark of the Unicorn's Digital Performer or Emagic Logic) will explain how to set up your sound sources (modules) and how to record separate tracks. If you need more information, there are many books and Web sites that include MIDI instruction. The quickest way to get set up is through the kindness of a friend who has a MIDI setup and can show you how to do it much more quickly than reading instruction books.

So, with very little expense, technical expertise, or musical instruction, millions of people become "desktop" composers/orchestrators. In choosing melodies, chords, and rhythms, they become composers, and, whether they realize it or not, in choosing electronic sounds for their MIDI computer compositions, they become orchestrators.

CHOOSING YOUR MIDI ORCHESTRA

Instruments chosen for a MIDI orchestra are limited only by the number of sounds in your computer library and recording tracks available in the sequencing program. Live orchestras are much more limited, so, if you plan to translate your MIDI files to a live band, choose your synth instruments to closely resemble the live band. And don't be seduced by the simple name assigned by the factory worker who assembled the synth sounds. If your "guitar" sound is better represented by what your music library lists as "harp-on-it," then by all means choose the MIDI instrument for its sound, not its name. Curiously, my sound module's biggest French horn section sound comes from a sound file labeled "small fr hn sec." So beware of these sometimes deceptive instrument labels. Maybe the trumpet sound you want is best achieved by selecting "tuba" and playing it in the trumpet range. Do some experimenting before settling on the best sounds for your band.

Let's suppose you are composing a film score and want to emulate the sound of a fairly good-sized recording orchestra:

> 2 flutes
> 2 oboes
> 2 clarinets
> 2 bassoons
>
> 4 French horns
> 3 trumpets
> 3 trombones
> 1 tuba
>
> 3 percussionists playing timpani, mallets, etc. (basically anything)
>
> piano
> harp
>
> 14 first violins
> 12 second violins
> 10 violas
> 8 celli
> 6 basses

The above order would be the way the instruments are traditionally displayed on the written score, but in MIDI-land there is no need to care about score order since MIDI files are mainly sound files. True, the sequencer programs usually include a "notation window" allowing you to look at the sounds as notes on typical five-line musical staves, but do not believe the blurb on the sequencer packaging that says you can print musical scores from your program. You need a professional music notation program (like Sibelius or Finale) to print professional-quality scores and parts for musicians. The order of the instrument tracks in the MIDI sequence results from the order of tracks entered as the composer starts composing—maybe a drum track or melodic line, followed by string chords, etc. Or, he could have a set template of instruments made up especially for the project to use for every cue. This is fine as long as the tracks are sound files. When creating a printed score for a live conductor, the various lines of instruments should be in the conventional "score order" listed above for any classically trained conductor to work with. The point is, this is a standard ordering for those familiar with orchestral scores, and maintaining that order saves time in the studio. If you have 20 film cues to record with a live band and each cue's score order is different, it can be disorienting for the conductor, and can cost valuable time.

WHY MIDI FILES LOOK SO STRANGE

When a musician who is accustomed to reading conventionally printed music first sees a part printed from a MIDI sequencer that has not been "cleaned up" (to look like conventional notation), he might be startled at how unusual it appears. The weird look of the music is through no fault of the composer who recorded it, but it reveals simply how MIDI sequencers "think."

First, every sequence must be given a tempo indication or it will default to quarter-note = 120 M.M. The performer recording the music has to hear this tempo click and play as rhythmically precise as possible. A MIDI sequencer is very sensitive to the human inaccuracies of rhythmic performance and notates *exactly* what it's told by the controller (MIDI keyboard). So, all manner of weird rhythms will usually appear, because people are not machines: 64th notes tied to 32nd notes, syncopations that were merely the player being too early for a certain beat, or melody notes that are held too long, creating tied notes. In general, many more notes than intended usually appear in the notation window. Before converting these MIDI tracks to notation for live players, they have to be "cleaned up." One way to do this is through "quantizing."

QUANTIZING

This feature in a sequencer program will correctly align the rhythm of what is played with respect to its correct rhythmic position in the measure. The player tells the program the smallest rhythmic value of the music, and the program will not allow any "smaller" rhythms to exist. If, for example, the smallest rhythmic value played is an eighth note, all those places where the player is early by a 64th note will simply be notated in the correct place right *on* the correct eighth note instead of before it. This feature can be turned on *before* recording so that the recording will be corrected as you play ("quantize on input"), or it can be done to a track after the recording is complete. Either way, it is essential to later notating the music correctly.

If your MIDI files will not be transferred to notation for a live player, but remain as an audio file, then you might not want to quantize everything, since it will align the rhythms so consistently that the music might sound inhumanly precise. That is something you will decide from the style of the music. Obviously, a very legato/rubato piano texture might not need any quantizing. But surely, a marching band piece with snare drums and very square rhythms could benefit greatly from quantizing where all the rhythms get locked together precisely.

IMPORT FILTERING

If you are importing your MIDI files into a notation program (such as Sibelius) you have the option of filtering what notes to import, whether you want to allow triplets, if so what kind, and what is the smallest rhythmic value you want to accept. It is a kind of quantizing but not called that.

TAPPING-IN BEATS

If a composer chooses, he can turn off the tempo click (metronone) in the MIDI sequence he is recording. The sequencer will then record whatever is played ("quantize on input" should be turned off) and the playback will sound exactly as played. Since the click was not audible for the recording, the click will be completely out of place from the music. This can be useful when a non-rigid, rubato feel is desired. But, before the music can be printed, the downbeats (all the first beats of the measures) must be aligned so they are really landing squarely on the first beats of measures to be read by a musician. To do this after a rubato track has already been played, there is a feature in the sequencer program that allows you, on playback of the rubato passage, to tap in the beats of the music as they go by in whatever irregular fashion they may be. Then when you look at the notation screen for that track, you will see it notated correctly with the downbeats where they should be. This can also be accomplished visually in a window that allows the pre-recorded music to be moved backward or forward to align the beats. It would be impossible to produce written parts for a live player from a rubato MIDI file if these quick-fix techniques were not available. (In Digital Performer version 3, these are called "record beats" and "adjust beats.")

TOO MANY TRACKS?

Having too many tracks is one of the most common reasons MIDI files cannot simply be printed for live performers to play. It is only natural for composers, in the heat of writing (recording MIDI tracks), to keep adding tracks. For example, a composer writing to a film scene might first play a slow violin melody while watching the video. Next, on a separate track, he might add some mid-range string "pads" (chords). Then, after getting an idea for a cello counter line, he adds that on another separate track. Each time he records, it is easiest to use a separate track. If he simply records again on the same track, the sequencer will automatically erase what was previously recorded. Thus, it is easy to see how one can accumulate ten to twelve string lines over the course of writing a cue. Since each of these tracks was recorded separately, each is on a separate stave when viewed in the notation window. Obviously, if this music is to be played by a live string orchestra, the ten or so string lines have to be condensed to the customary five in order to be playable.

The MIDI composer must realize that there is a limit to how many different lines a string orchestra can play. On the synthesizer, the more layers of string parts you play, the bigger the string sound. With a live string section the *opposite* is true. The more you divide a limited number of strings, the weaker each divided section becomes. If 20 violins are to play two lines then ten violins play each line, no problem. But if those same 20 players are expected to play three or four different lines, then we are going to lose power on each, ending up with maybe five players per line. This is a difference that will be readily noticed, especially if the music at this point needs to be loud. You can do more "divisi" (divided string parts) with soft music but if you divide them excessively for loud passages, it will sound very different from the MIDI version you are used to— thinner sounding, because the synth sound is additive and the live string divisi is not.

Having too many tracks can happen in any area of the MIDI orchestra. It frequently happens with percussion sounds. When adding sounds (e.g., a bass drum hit, then a cymbal crash, etc.), each new sound requires its own separate track, because it is a different patch. It's up to the orchestrator to reduce the excess tracks to the appropriate number for live performers. I remember being given 17 percussion tracks in a MIDI file that was to be played with 6 live percussionists. I combined the parts as much as I could, but we still had to do percussion overdubs after the main orchestra had gone.

STANDARD MIDI FILE FORMAT

Once your MIDI files have been recorded to your satisfaction and are ready to be sent to a standard notation program for the preparation of a printed score and separate parts for the live players, you must save them in the "Standard MIDI File format." This format is easily read by most computer music programs, and a MIDI file has a standard suffix, ".mid".

MIDI data itself is rather nondescript, offering info about which keys were held and for how long, mainly a series of on-off commands. The actual sound that this data assumes is determined by its destination, which means the same MIDI file can be "interpreted" differently with each new setup it encounters. This allows a composer to assign whatever patch (synth sound) he chooses to a single musical track recorded in the MIDI file. The MIDI file itself is not sound-specific and can be used with any patch you choose. Your electronic "string quartet" can, with a few quick keystrokes, become an electronic "brass quartet." This can also cause great difficulty if you wish to re-create the exact sound of your MIDI setup by taking your MIDI files to another MIDI setup because there are so many variables between workstations. It is not wise to attempt it unless you have many hours to make sure both setups are the same.

Also, MIDI files do not have any visual articulation or dynamic markings associated with them, which means a Standard MIDI File opened in the Sibelius notation program will simply show the pitches of the notes played and their durations. No slurs for legato notes or dots indicating staccato for short notes or dynamics. These must be added. A staccato note will simply have a very short duration (e.g., 32nd or 64th note) and must be changed to an eighth note with a dot over it for a more typical appearance. You can have Sibelius' input filter interpret all very short notes as eighths with dots, but you cannot have it automatically put in slurs for what was played as legato, smoothly connected notes. These must be entered manually, along with all dynamics.

Tempo markings (e.g., quarter note = 112) will be included in a Standard MIDI File, so when it is opened in Sibelius every tempo change will appear at the top of the score. If there are not too many of these I perfer to leave them in the players' parts when they are printed for an exact description of tempo. When there are too many, as in a ritard where a blur of markings are automatically entered, I manually eliminate all but a few.

Meter signatures ($\frac{4}{4}$, $\frac{3}{4}$, etc.) are also maintained in the MIDI file transfer. Key signatures will be as well, *if* they are entered in the original sequence and saved. If not, there will be a random spelling of accidentals (sharps and flats) that will have to be made consistent with the key signature.

The proper notation of triplets can be a problem for Standard MIDI File transfers. The file will no doubt *sound* correct, but when the notation program opens it, the triplets may have any number of unusual rhythms. If these strange rhythms do not occur very often in a piece, I simply listen to my audio dub of it (or listen to the file itself) and confirm what the correct rhythm should be and fix it manually. If it is a widespread problem throughout a long piece, I will try various parameters of the Sibelius input filter until it opens the rhythms correctly.

Opening a Standard MIDI File in Sibelius you get the default "optimized score," where only those staves of the MIDI orchestra containing notes are shown. It is important to change this to show all staves, even empty ones, before working so no tracks of music are overlooked.

In general, you must check the Standard MIDI Files closely with another source, such as an audio dub, to be sure the MIDI file hasn't misinterpreted something. For example, I have seen one notation program consistently leave out the held notes of a "pyramid" chord structure when being played into the sequencer, where chord tones are added on top of one another and all are sustained. It shows only the new pitches as they are added, so without checking another source, this would be notated for the players incorrectly as an arpeggio. MIDI files are a great way to exchange performance data, but they can be unpredictable at times.

MIDI CAN DO THE "IMPOSSIBLE"

The more you know about traditional instrumental orchestration, the better equipped you will be to avoid printing parts that cannot be played by live musicians. The following are things that MIDI can do but live players cannot:

1. **MIDI can make all instruments audible no matter what range they may be in.** You may have a low flute solo in a MIDI file that sounds louder than the rest of the orchestra, but this is not a realistic balance, since real flutes get very soft the lower they play and would be covered by the orchestra. You can double woodwinds on top of brass in a MIDI file and still hear them, but it's not likely with a live orchestra because the brass is so much stronger.

2. **MIDI can make tricky rhythms perfectly in sync throughout the orchestra.** This is only possible in varying degrees from live band to live band, but the point is, if your MIDI file was "quantized" (rhythmically aligned in perfect sync) there is simply no live band that can emulate that, nor would they want to. Live music gets its individuality from the little

imperfections coming from various parts of the orchestra, and this is good, up to a point.

3. **MIDI can sound bigger than live instruments.** Because of its power, a single brass patch (trumpet, trombone, or French horn) can sound huge and totally sufficient in a MIDI situation, but in a live orchestra, one trumpet could not produce the same power a synth can and more brass instruments need to be added to fill out the brass section sound. Synth patches (especially strings) can be made up of several layered sounds, maybe with octaves and reverb included. It frequently happens that synth string emulations sound bigger than the actual live string orchestra if the composer is not careful to keep his synth patches realistic when emulating the live band.

4. **MIDI can have perfect intonation throughout the instrument ranges.** Orchestrators learn that certain parts of an instrument's range are more difficult to play in tune than others (e.g., very high notes on all instruments, especially strings), yet this is not apparent on a synth. Very high woodwinds in thirds is difficult for live players, but no problem on the synth. Everything sounds equally in tune (or out, depending on the patches used).

5. **MIDI can play outside the live instruments' range.** Fortunately, some notation programs, like Sibelius, will tell you when you have exceeded an instrument's normal range by coloring the notes red. A MIDI composer needs to know live instrument ranges to be sure his parameters are set correctly in his notation program (they can be altered). If he plays a synth French horn in the high trumpet range, will he like the sound of the trumpet that will have to play it? Maybe the flugelhorn will do, or a trumpet with a flugelhorn mouthpiece.

6. **MIDI needs fewer musical elements to sound complete.** It takes experience to appreciate this, and knowledge of orchestration, but "synth space" is more easily filled than "live orchestra space." This means that two to three lines in a MIDI orchestra emulation can sound very adequate, but in translation, live orchestras often need more texture, more contrapuntal motion, or inner parts to keep it interesting.

7. **MIDI can emulate brass and woodwind sounds that never need to breathe.** It is easy to forget, while playing your synth, that when these parts are put before live musicians, the extremely long notes may have to be interrupted by the wind players taking breaths. If it is necessary to maintain long lines, and you have at least two players covering one part, they can dovetail or stagger their breathing to make pauses for breath nearly unnoticeable, but that requires sufficient players. Strings, of course, do not have this problem. A possible remedy if you do not have enough players is to mix in some quality synth sounds along with the live players. (These synth sounds should be available for the live players to tune to when they play).

8. **MIDI strings sound bigger as more lines are added.** If a live string section is asked to divide its players into many lines (divisi) then the sound of each line becomes weaker. But in a MIDI emulation of a string section, a divided string section sounds bigger with each new line added, simply because there are more notes sounding. This, along with the rotund quality of some string patches, is a good reason why there is sometimes disappointment at the sound of a live string orchestra, compared to a MIDI version.

A good "reality check" for a composer and his MIDI sequencing setup would be to take a classical piece for which he has a CD recording and the printed score (say for a Mozart symphony). Enter a portion of the printed score into the sequencer and see how close you can come to emulating the sound of the CD. Granted, there will always be variables on the CD of room acoustics, mics the engineer used, how many strings, and especially tempo variations, etc., but it will surely let you know if you are speaking the same language as the acoustic orchestral world.

WHAT MIDI CANNOT DO

As every hero has his Achilles heel, so MIDI has its limits in emulating live orchestral instruments. We just spoke of those things that MIDI can do that far exceed the limits of live instruments. Below are things that live players can do but MIDI cannot:

1. **MIDI cannot produce the sound of four very loud unison trumpets.** If four tracks of MIDI use the same trumpet patch, the sound

of a MIDI unison will often sound weaker than just one track because the phasing of the unison sounds tends to cancel each other out, thereby diminishing the overall sound. Whereas, in a live orchestra, there is almost nothing stronger than the sound of four unison trumpets because their volume is additive. This diminished volume effect may apply to other brass patches, as well.

2. **MIDI cannot reflect different sound qualities throughout an instrument's range.** A bassoon in real life has a sharp edge to its lower register that can sometimes be used to comic effect. But, when it gets up around middle "C" it becomes a beautifully round sound almost like a small French horn. (Remember the opening to Stravinsky's "The Rite of Spring.") "Sampled" sounds are better able to reflect an instruments color changes, if each note is sampled.

3. **MIDI cannot reflect those combinations of instruments that clash.** For example, an acoustic clarinet and oboe have difficulty in blending their very disparate sounds, yet on the synth we would never know this. Also, a live tuba and bass trombone, while both capable of playing many notes in unison, don't have the same kind of tone color and are often found in octaves and fifths in live orchestras.

4. **MIDI cannot emulate the strings' natural tendency to be expressive.** I have known composers who actually get upset when live strings do not sound exactly like their synth counterparts (where there is no crescendo at the beginnings of lines and diminuendo at the end, no change of vibrato, etc.) There are so many things indigenous to strings that cannot be reflected in a synth emulation. It is good to get away from your synth sounds occasionally and experience live instruments so you *do not expect players to emulate your synth;* <u>it's supposed to be the other way around!</u>

5. **MIDI cannot easily change its manner of performance.** A conductor can ask musicians to play a piece again but with a "more playful" approach, or the opposite, to play something "more seriously with more of a somber or sustained quality." The computer only speaks the language of the program used, and while changes in the manner of performance of a MIDI file are possible, they can take a lot of time to accomplish and the outcome is never guaranteed.

6. **MIDI cannot reflect the physical limitations of certain instruments.** The physical problems associated with producing extremely low, high, or long notes in live woodwinds or brass can go unnoticed in a synth mockup. I have seen brass expected to hold low notes for eight to ten measures in a slow tempo, the composer being unaware that live musicians are not capable of that. Knowledge of orchestration can save time fixing such problems in the studio.

7. **MIDI cannot easily reflect an unequal string divisi.** There are times when two string parts on one line are divided between the players of that line (e.g., first violins), and this is normally a 50-50 split. But live musicians can be asked to have two-thirds of the players play the top line and only one-third play the bottom line for a different balance in a certain passage. Synth mockups rarely get to this level of sophistication.

8. **MIDI scores do not often have two or more different sounds on the same track.** It is usually most convenient for separate sounds to be distributed to different MIDI tracks. With timpani, for example, the rolled notes occur on a line separate from the struck notes. These two sounds can be incorporated into one track, but the result of the MIDI notation might show them in two different octaves. The wrong octave placement can happen with any instrument, and in MIDI transfers it is something to keep an eye on.

9. **MIDI cannot produce contemporary orchestration techniques.** Depending on the sound sources you are using, chances are that you will be limited in the number of contemporary orchestration effects you can use in your MIDI mockup. Sounds such as strings playing on the "wrong side of the bridge," or light harmonic glissandi, or brass just blowing air through their instruments, etc., will probably not be available as MIDI sounds. More and more sampled sounds are becoming available, but for now, if you wish to try these effects, you had better have alternative sounds programmed into your MIDI sequence, and then, at the recording session, dictate these effects to the orchestra (or have alternate parts ready) to try for the director's approval. Maybe they will work, and maybe not.

The differences between the MIDI orchestra and the *live* orchestra can be more easily summarized by the following chart:

	MIDI orchestra	live orchestra
all instruments audible no matter what range they may be in:	yes	no
tricky rhythms perfectly in sync throughout the orchestra:	yes	no
sound bigger than live instruments:	yes	no
perfect intonation throughout their ranges:	yes	no
play outside the live instrument's range:	yes	no
endless breath for wind instruments:	yes	no
string subdivisions with no loss of sound:	yes	no
realistic sound of four loud unison trumpets:	no	yes
varied sound qualities throughout an instrument's range:	no	yes
reflect clashes between instrumental tone colors:	no	yes
expressive string performance:	no	yes
open to interpretive performances:	no	yes
reflect the physical limitations of instruments:	no	yes
unequal string divisi:	no	yes
have one player change sounds:	maybe	yes
play contemporary techniques:	no	yes

The pitfalls in the transfer of MIDI files to live orchestra are many and can be different with each MIDI file. Your best guide through the transition is a knowledge of traditional orchestration, which, granted, is tough to come by these days. First-hand experience is primary for understanding the capabilities and special qualities of each live instrument. I can only suggest that you take every opportunity to experience the sound of whatever instruments you can. Try alternative orchestration nuances when you have a live orchestra at your disposal. If you have no live recording sessions to experiment with, survey your live musical environment to see if there are musicians (in any configuration) to play your music—a string quartet, solo instruments, a high school band, a small jazz group. Your main objective should be to learn as much about the instruments in any way you can so that you become a thoughtful and effective orchestrator of your own music.

Obviously, until you reach that stage, you may need help from a professional orchestrator. Do not hesitate to ask for advice, even if you can't pay them for their time. They are usually congenial types who will no doubt be glad to comment on your scores. You might want to treat them to lunch while they look at your work.

And most importantly, listen to live music (such as symphony orchestra rehearsals, whether professional or amateur) with score in hand when possible. And, when not, listen to an orchestral CD with the score to follow note for note. The more associations you make between the printed score and the live sound, the better. This is the key to effective orchestration and it will enable you to not only emulate the scores that you study, but to eventually choose your own personal orchestrational preferences, or even invent new ones.

Orchestration 5

*T*oday, a beginning film composer usually starts off by purchasing a computer and a sequencing program that can lock to VHS tape or import QuickTime video files. The locking to film might come only after he sees first-hand how laborious it is to manually locate start points for each playback, and experiences the need to precisely coordinate video and sound for synching hit points. The new film composer's venture into the world of orchestration may begin in the music store when he decides which sound module or software samples to buy for his orchestral emulations. The more sounds in his library, the larger his palette of musical color. If the composer has little experience with orchestral music, these same sound modules will influence his compositional choices as well. If the composer has no "pizzicato string" sound, for example, that color will not be available to him and will not exist in his mental sound universe as a possibility, unless he already knows of it. It is important for a composer to be aware of his synthesizer's color limitations and expand them through classical score reading and listening. Even the most elaborate sound modules do not yet include some contemporary string effects such as "light harmonic glissandi" or playing on the "wrong side of the bridge," etc.

Fortunately for live musicians, purely electronic sounds indigenous to synthesizers have not yet flooded the film composer vocabularies. In fact, if we hear a common synth sound in a film score, those who know what it is are less than impressed. What we hear in most feature scores are real orchestral instruments that have been around for centuries, and the synth mockups for these scores depend mostly on emulating these age-old live instruments. Enter the orchestrator.

Until Hollywood imposed its tight schedules, it was common for film composers to also orchestrate their music. For probably the last 50 years or so we have seen orchestration breaking away from the film composing process as a separate entity out of necessity. Budgets and schedules shrink, meaning less time for the composer to work. A few film composers still orchestrate their own scores, e.g., Howard Shore and Ennio Morricone; John Williams' sketches are so complete they are nearly orchestrations. Nevertheless, until budding young composers follow the little green brick road to the land of blockbuster budgets, they will likely be their own orchestrators and it is in their best interest to become as familiar as possible with what orchestration is and how their knowledge of it can enhance their music.

So that your own little world of synth patches doesn't trap you into a corner, the best way to familiarize yourself with the capabilities of the orchestra is to listen to classical CDs *with* the score. There are even some John Williams scores available through Hal Leonard publishers for a look at a very big Hollywood sound. You probably won't start out writing for orchestras this large, but you should prepare ahead of time. Listen and look, over and over again, just 20 or 30 bars at a time, until you know every inch of it. Follow each instrument to get a feeling for what kind of music it plays best; notice their ranges and tone qualities, both high and low. If you can hire an orchestrator to help you with your score, ask him why he does what he does and compare his scores with the end result of your recording and your original MIDI files. If you develop an interest in orchestration, you will find an endless source of joy and discovery in the classical scores of the past. Begin with simpler music, like Haydn or Mozart symphonies and progress toward the present day slowly. (For more on the study of scoring, see Chapter Ten, Practice.).

COLOR

The subject of orchestral color has filled innumerable books. I only hope to call the beginning composer's attention to the dramatic power orchestral color can make and how, by changing color alone, you also change the interpretation of the scene. The MIDI sequencer can illustrate this very simply. If you have a slow, four-part, quarter-note texture, it might seem most appropriate in mid-range strings. But if you condense the texture as closely as possible and put it up two octaves in a purely violin color, it suddenly goes from a pastoral feel to one of saintly ascension. Or if you take this same condensed version down three octaves in a low brass color, you have another totally different version that is dark with an ominous tone—very different emotions from the same music.

When you hear the zither in the film *The Third Man*, the ondes martenot in *The Grifters*, or the bold sound of the brass for the jousting scenes in *A Knight's*

Tale, you can see what a powerful effect instrumental color can have on the mood of the score. Jerry Goldsmith, a composer who probably conceives the color of the orchestration along with his musical themes, acknowledges the power of pure color alone when he says, "Anyone with any kind of technique can make an orchestra sound marvelous for two hours even without any musical content." That power of the orchestral sound to overwhelm plays to the composer's advantage when a first-time director hears the score. What may have been dissatisfaction with a synth mockup often disappears when the director hears it with a live orchestra.

PICKING THE BAND

Choosing the right instruments that will faithfully reproduce your synth mockup should be done with an orchestrator, who is more familiar with the capabilities of live instruments. If your synth score had just one high brass line, this doesn't mean you hire only one trumpet. Nor should you do like one first-time film composer, who, when asked by the contractor what band he wanted, replied, "Just get one of everything." What an impossible band that would be to balance.

MIDI scores that are translated into live scores need adjustments of balance, usually by filling out what was originally too few parts. I remember being given an orchestra to write for that was complete in its traditional complement of players except it had no trumpets. In order to balance the brass section, I asked for three trumpets but was careful not to use them prominently, as that was not in the composer's concept.

While it's true that in a recording studio it's possible to do the "impossible," i.e., make a low flute the lead melody in the context of a full orchestral accompaniment, it is more expedient to write as though you were playing live so there are not special balances for each cue at the mixing session. The old orchestration adage of "balance each section within itself" is a good general approach. Woodwinds, brass, and strings should sound balanced when played separately. This also allows you to maintain a balance in case a director wants to eliminate all the brass, for example.

If you choose the following band, you will be disappointed in the predominance of brass (unless you like that sound or choose to use a lot of brass mutes):

1 fl, 1 ob, 1 cl, 1 bsn
3 tpts, 3 trbs, tuba, 4 hns
10 violin I, 8 violin II, 6 violas, 4 celli, 2 bass

This would be a more typical balance:

> 1 fl, 1 ob, 1 cl, 1 bsn
> 1 tpt, 1 trb, 2 hns
> 10 violin I, 8 violin II, 6 violas, 4 celli, 2 bass

Don't hire too many players, even if you have the budget for it. The number of brass required can determine the size of the rest of the orchestra, because the more brass you have, the more woodwinds and strings you need to counterbalance them. Another way the brass can affect an orchestration is if the last chord needs a certain quality of having the first trumpet at the top of its range, the key of the orchestration is determined by that last first trumpet note.

The traditional symphonic orchestra complement of strings can include eight contrabasses or more, but rarely do you need more than six basses in a typical studio recording situation. If you are in a large acoustic space that is used for live concerts and there is a lot of echo, you might want a larger string section to fill the hall. These are things only an experienced orchestrator would know, so trust him in helping you choose the right balance.

Also, it is worth noting that smaller bands are not always easier to orchestrate. In fact, the reverse is usually true. I found the score for *Spanish Prisoner* more challenging in that regard simply because when the band was smaller due to budget restrictions, each instrument became more important in the overall sound.

USING YOUR SEQUENCER AT THE SESSION

The most common use of the sequencer is of course producing mockups of the orchestra for the director to hear with the film, prior to the recording sessions. This is almost always expected, except when the composer is very famous or has a long-standing working relationship with the director. I doubt if John Williams has to do mockups for Steven Spielberg.

At the recording session, sequencer tracks played on a laptop computer usually provide the click track for the orchestra. Having the original sequences on hand also enables the composer to play along with the orchestra whatever indigenous electronic sounds he has used in the score, along with possibly doubling some live instruments for added strength (usually strings). For example, in *A Knights Tale*, Carter Burwell doubled the live strings with synth strings that had a "swimmy," underwater quality that was appropriate for a very foggy, mysterious mood.

The sequencer can also be used to play for the director those instrumental parts that are missing as the live orchestra is playing. For whatever reason, you must sometimes have certain instruments, typically percussion, overdubbed at later sessions. It is important for the director to hear all parts so he can understand the intent of the cue on the first playing. The composer plays his MIDI sequence in the studio but only turns on those tracks whose parts are temporarily missing in the orchestral performance.

Then there is the use of the sequencer to perform the entire film score. While perhaps cost effective, it is a compromise at best. My compliments to those composers who go out of their way to use live orchestras. They could undoubtedly make more money with a purely synth score, but prefer the live orchestral sound when possible and are willing to pay for it.

UNUSUAL INSTRUMENTS

Finding unusual ethnic instruments is another way for a composer to put a unique stamp on a score. Film composers will often go to great lengths to show how original they can be.

To use an oud, sitar, or some other non-traditional instrument in a prominent way can be very effective. Just be aware, ethnic instruments tend to have very limited ranges and/or keys. Be sure to talk with the player in advance as to what the instrument's limitations are and how he would like the part to be written. The weirdest one I ever saw was the highland bagpipe, which had to be written in the key of "A" but sounded in "B♭." I faxed the part to the player in advance to be sure there were no problems. The last thing you want at a session is a part that's impossible to play. If the key of the orchestration needs to be changed to accommodate an unusual instrument, simply check with the composer to see if the original key is movable. He might have a reason that would make a key change undesirable.

SLURS AND STRING BOWINGS

In my experience in writing for recording sessions I have come to realize the most efficient way to mark phrasings for woodwinds and strings (even legato brass) is to simply write the word "legato" rather than put in the slurs, except for shorter ones that are tutti. Some judiciously placed rests can delineate the phrase structure. I have learned that a really good woodwind player is capable of much more breath than you might expect. I remember a bass clarinet player asking me if I wanted him to continue a line in the manner of the strings, which of course don't have to breathe. I said, "Sure," and he proceeded to play with breathing I would have thought impossible. I now write very long lines for woodwinds on occasion with a note that they can breathe at will, since they are by far the best judges of that.

A similar situation exists with strings, where concertmasters have told me they much prefer the simple word "legato," letting them figure out the bowings. It's more practical, too, as it becomes awkward in music notation programs to indicate long slurs neatly. They seem to get in the way of other things, so I now leave them out with no deleterious effects.

CLEFS AND TRANSPOSING INSTRUMENTS

Most commercial music composers who write for film, jingles, or pop artists and create scores on paper, use "C" or "concert" scores, which show the pitches of almost all instruments where they actually sound (except for bass, glock, piccolo, guitar, etc., which have an octave or two transposition that would yield too many ledger lines). On the other hand, most classically trained composers use transposed scores, which show the instruments notated in their transposed keys as they appear on the player's part. The use of either type of score does not in itself suggest one composer is any more capable than the other. However, a beginning writer should know the pros and cons of each.

The traditional transpositions of the instruments, though always unpleasant for new orchestration students to learn, accomplish one very important thing. They keep the primary music for those instruments in one staff without many ledger lines. You will notice on "C" scores that certain instruments will need many ledger lines or a frequent changing of clefs to accommodate all the notes of their range on one stave. If you take the advice of those who suggest writing viola in treble clef, you will have to frequently change from treble to bass clefs or use many ledger lines. Also, the copyist will have to transpose the part, which could add another chance for error into the process.

Lower French horn parts in "C" scores will also have lots of ledger lines or have to frequently change back and forth between treble and bass clefs if not given the fifth transposition. There is also a tendency in "C" scores for the beginner to write the French horns too high, forgetting that the part has its pitches transposed up a perfect 5th.

The use of "C" scores gives the copyist more to fix in preparing the parts. For example, bari sax or bass clarinet parts, when changed from the bass clef of the concert score to the treble clef of the transposed score, require a bit of formatting in a notation program because the stems often change direction, which in turn affects slurs and dynamics which have to be adjusted. This is, however, unavoidable if the composer requests a "C" score.

The biggest annoyance I find with "C" scores is the discrepancy between the appearance of that instrument on the score and on the part when a question arises. Granted, these are not insurmountable problems, just something else to eat up valuable time at a session.

As for viola, there are some advocates of writing its music in treble clef, which will, like other instruments mentioned, produce unnecessary ledger lines or frequent changes from treble to bass clef. Viola should always be written in alto clef for both transposed and "C" scores. It is simply unprofessional to do otherwise.

I feel strongly that when you choose to write for the traditional symphonic orchestra, you are coming to play on the players' turf, and you should familiarize yourself with the language of the orchestra. It's much like going to a foreign country and learning its language to help your understanding of the deeper meanings of the culture. Learning the transpositions and clefs is not as difficult as you may think, if you give it a little time. After all, young children can learn alto clef very quickly because they lack the confusion with what we more experienced musicians see as the popular treble and bass clefs. Also, a very important benefit of a familiarity with transposed scores is that it creates a window into the classical scores of the past, which is an orchestrator's greatest source of information about his craft.

PRINTED SCORES

Scores larger than 20 lines or so should be formatted for legal size paper, which is 8.5 x 14 inches, and they can be enlarged easily to 11 x 17 for the conductor. Also, it is incumbent upon the orchestrator to include everything necessary for the extraction of parts on the score, showing all dynamics, slurs, articulation marks, etc. You should not expect the copyist to have to fix each part individually, because when the push is on and time is short, you might end up with incomplete parts that you'll have to spend valuable time correcting at the session. For example, it may be inconvenient for you to include dynamics for each instrument in a tutti section. Learn how to do it, maybe using "Quick Keys" or your own macros. But do not expect the copyist to do this for you. In the old days, when copyists hand-copied scores, they could look out for such things, but now with computerized part extraction, it is chancy to expect all this information to appear in the parts unless the orchestrator puts it there.

Assume that your scores will be self-explanatory and your absence from the sessions will not impair their reading. It is always nice to be there if you can, to remind the orchestra of certain things and enjoy the fruits of your labor, but if you can't, nothing should be left unaccounted for. If you know in advance you will not be at the session (either because of scheduling, budgetary, or other reasons), you can type in text notes on the scores for the conductor, pointing out certain things like inner lines or tricky doublings. You can make notes to the mixer on the score as well when a soft instrument like harp has an important part that must be heard. Someone in the booth will have a score and can relate this to him, or he might see it himself if he follows the score.

MODULATIONS

In the interest of not wasting any time at the recording session, I have found that if the music changes key frequently, every two bars or so, the writing in of new key signatures can create problems. Since we are dealing with a sight-reading environment, it will serve you well *not* to change key signatures for the short term but only do it for major sections. Apparently it is easier for the players to read accidentals than remember key changes.

TEMPO CHANGES

If the orchestrator receives a MIDI file from the composer, chances are the tempo changes will be transferred in conventional metronome markings. I instruct the copyist to leave these in the parts because they are sometimes radically shifting up and down, and the actual M.M. numbers can give the player a more accurate clue of what is happening than the more general "accel" or "ritard." The exception is a MIDI ritard, where there will be a flood of tempo changes shown—obviously these should be reduced to just a few and the word "ritard" needs to be added to the score.

SYNTH PITFALLS

The ultimate MIDI challenge would be to emulate the sound of four trumpets playing a unison melody. In fact, with MIDI, when you create four separate tracks of trumpets playing in unison, the phasing of the patches cancels out some of the sound so that the result is actually *weaker* than just one trumpet track. Another pitfall of MIDI orchestrations is that occasionally a track will be in the wrong octave. This is usually apparent from listening to the audio dub the composer gives you of his sequence, or simply by seeing the inordinate number of ledger lines that appear.

Also, when strings are written divisi (more than one line per stave) the synth version will sound fuller because of the added notes. However, with a live string orchestra, divisi parts will *reduce* the overall volume due to fewer players per line. Beware of the fullness of a synth string divisi part and allow for the lack of power by possibly adding reinforcement with other instruments, such as horns, if more sound is required.

One of the worst temptations in working with synth scores in general is the allure of copying and pasting previous sections of a score for reoccurring sections or cues later on. It is always wise to do at least some modifications that will be apparent to the listener and refreshing to the ear. Especially simple changes for computers are modulations, simply taking some instruments out, or changing a melody from one instrumental color to another.

BIG SOUND, SMALL BAND

If you have a few cues for which a bigger sound is desirable, you can (under AFM union rules) overdub these cues at another session for no extra charge (doing it at the same session will cost double). So, if you wish to double the size of your string section, for example, you can record the basic track at one session and overdub them at a later session. To do this for every cue is not a productive approach, but it can help for a few important cues if you have budget restrictions.

Even if your score begins and ends electronically, never seeing paper or a live orchestra, going from MIDI sketch to MIDI orchestration to MIDI final dub, the study of live orchestration can definitely help your awareness of orchestral color and balance.

Conducting

Many beginning composers shy away from conducting their own film scores, which is like a carpenter who only makes tabletops but not legs. Conducting should be as much a part of the process of creating a film score as the composing. Every composer, whether formally trained or not, should at least give it a fair try, for several reasons:

1. The composer knows what he wants to hear, and maybe the fastest way to get it is for him to conduct.

2. By having the "best seat in the house," the composer will experience the live orchestral sound in such an intimate way that it will build his aural memory of what works best and his future scores will benefit greatly.

3. It enables a more personal contact with the players; the performance suggestions they offer can be filed away for future reference.

4. It helps establish a common ground between the composer and players, much the same as a director who acts.

5. The musical perspective from the podium is different from that of the booth, and that can be good.

6. When the players have questions, they would much rather hear answers from the composer than from anyone else. They aim to please, especially the person who is responsible for giving them the gig.

So many beginners feel they have to pretend to be a better conductor than they really are, or they will be "found out" and lose the respect of the players. The exact opposite is true. If you make an honest effort to be clear with your instructions and beat, and are not pretentious, you will be amazed how helpful the players can be. Recording musicians are used to *all* kinds of conductors, and if you are merely efficient, they will give you a good performance and not expect you to be Erich Leinsdorf. Listen closely as you go, marking places with a red pen for comments to the players before the next take. The orchestra acts as a mirror of your personality. If you are sincerely happy to be there, they will reflect the same feeling because they do want to please you. So enjoy the moment—it can truly be thrilling.

One of the biggest thrills I ever had conducting came with the film *Hudsucker Proxy*. The opening credits, a slow three-minute cue without click as we approached the visual climax of a clock's second hand sweeping up to 12. We were building an orchestral crescendo and accelerando, ready to zero in on the final big moment when the hand hit 12, and we nailed it; what a kick that was.

If you are the composer, this is your show. You are the reason all these people have gathered here, and it can be better than playing back the best synth mockup you've ever done. If you feel a need for a conducting course, take one and ease into it. There are many books on conducting; two very good ones for beginners are *The Grammar of Conducting* by Max Rudolf and *The Art of Conducting* by Donald Hunsberger and Roy Ernst. Hopefully, you will reach that feeling of "dancing as though no one were watching" when you get on the conductor's podium.

In fact, if you are a dancer, it doesn't hurt to think of the conductor as someone who is dancing to the music. This can really help to give the players the feeling you want from them. Jump up if you are excited and jab at the celli for more of an attack if you feel like it. Leonard Bernstein was often criticized for being overly emotional on the podium, but I always felt that he was feeling the music in a very deep way that made him move the way he did, for he had gestures that no other conductor had, and he would *smile* at times. This let us know he was having as good a time as we were. Don't be too serious. Some film score composers are certainly not trained conductors, but the musicians love to play for them simply because they are enjoying the moment. I hear that Randy Newman's sessions are great fun.

Then, after you've given it a shot, if you still prefer to hire a conductor, at least you have first-hand knowledge of what is taking place on the podium and what to expect from your conductor. If you choose not to conduct, the next best choice for a conductor is probably the orchestrator, since he is familiar with your music and you can then be in the booth with the director. If the director is new to the recording situation, or is unsure about how each cue should be handled, the composer can help guide him through.

And last, if the band is fewer than ten musicians and your music has a pulse to it (maybe even a drum set player), then you will not need a conductor at all. Simply give them a bar or two of count-off and let them go, while you listen from the booth.

KNOW THE FILM

Hopefully the composer will have no trouble with this, but if you are not the composer, familiarize yourself as much as possible with the video. The more you watch it, the more you will notice little things—an actor moving his hand on a viola entrance, places where the music is background and then moves to the foreground, etc. All manner of nuance will become apparent. Perhaps you might want to conduct to the video as you listen to the composer's synth mockups. If there is a click (which will usually be the case) maybe ask the composer to give you just that to practice with. The composer Georges Delerue was a master of conducting his scores without click, streamers, or clock. He was not flashy at all, but very involved in the music, and he knew the film so well that the score and the screen became one, and the players loved him for it.

Assuming you are willing to take the plunge into conducting your first session, here are some tips.

COMMUNICATING WITH THE DIRECTOR

Directors are almost always present at the recording sessions, as they are anxious to hear the final product and the sheer sound of the orchestra is usually very exciting for them. So if you are the composer and are conducting, you need to consider beforehand how best to communicate with the director after each take. With a big budget and lots of time, there is no problem. You simply walk into the booth after each take and discuss it upon playback to film with the director, with dialog if he wants. Even the players might be brought in to listen to a playback that involves them in an important way. It is both a courtesy and helpful to get their comments about nuances you may be discussing with the director. If time and money are limited you might want to simply ask for an okay from the booth after a successful take, keep moving, and listen to playbacks later after the orchestra has gone, re-doing any problematic cues later. This is not the ideal way to work, but if necessary, it can be done.

PLANNING THE RECORDING ORDER

Usually the biggest cues are played first, with respect to their thematic content and orchestration. Obviously, once the band is rehearsed for one cue, then doing similar ones immediately after it will facilitate the process. (If a group of cues require a lot of rehearsal and will be recorded over more than a single session, the contractor should be consulted to see if the same players will be returning to the following sessions, otherwise you'll have to rehearse the concept again with the new players.)

Consider the psychological effect of the first cue you record. It always takes the longest because the mixer is getting the board set up and adjusting levels and getting used to the room, etc. If it's a very long and difficult cue with lots of percussion, tempo changes, and wide-ranging dynamics, it could be too frustrating for everyone as a first choice. Also, it is likely that you won't finish it in one session. Better to choose a first cue that uses the full orchestra and one that is relatively easy to complete (although not as short as a two- to three-bar stinger). Everyone feels better after getting a first, fairly substantial cue or two done. Then you can go on to the more difficult ones with a positive mindset. The following cues will go much faster. You can usually plan to record seven to ten minutes of score per three-hour session, including the mandatory union breaks of ten minutes per hour. Even more can be done if the music is simple, but this is a good starting estimate. European sessions, notably Prague, have fewer breaks, with only one or two breaks per four-hour session.

If you wish to continue recording and the break time is upon you, consult with the contractor about possibly playing through one break and making it up later.

ABOUT BATONS

First-time conductors might feel awkward using a baton to conduct, but the benefits to the orchestra are worth your discomfort. They are used to seeing batons. It simply increases their field of view of the beat by the length of the stick. If you think about it, they are used to seeing batons against a dark background of a black tuxedo or the dark background of the concert hall. In a well-lighted studio, a white baton in front of a white shirt that is in front of a white wall is nearly lost. It may sound like a silly notion, but you can enhance the players' view of the baton by simply wearing a dark shirt. This was proven to me (upon watching myself conduct on video tape) on a day that I had worn a black shirt, and the white baton was clearly visible. It was so striking, I even considered, for variety, getting a black baton for the following day and wearing a white shirt.

PREPARE THE ORCHESTRA BEFORE PLAYING

Before beginning the rehearsal of any cue, call the players' attention to any ritards, accelerandos, or generally tricky spots and show them how you intend to conduct these sections. Walk them through any tempo changes to make sure that all those in the score also appear in their parts. Mention places where there are important doublings where they may need to listen more closely to their accompanying player, and in general, any balance considerations. Review also any abrupt dynamic changes. You might want to describe to them briefly what is happening on the video if it might enhance their performance, but don't go overboard, as lengthy descriptions can bring on a glassy-eyed response and less than enthusiastic performance. If their appreciation of the video is really important, maybe you should consider having a video projection for the orchestra as well.

After rehearsing a cue once or twice without click, consult with the mixer about which groups of instruments he would like to begin balancing (violins, woodwinds, brass, etc.) until all are ready to record. For brass, having them play a chord in "pyramid" fashion is a good way to hear the balance, or simply choose a section where all the players of that section are playing.

The conductor must wait for a verbal cue from the mixer, in the form of the "slate," meaning the recorded announcement of which cue and which take is coming up. This facilitates locating takes later at the mixing session.

Unbelievable as it may seem, there are times when certain players will be disruptive to the recording process by talking, joking around, and wasting valuable time. The conductor need not try to fix this; he may simply have the contractor take care of it. I have even seen young players who, for whatever reason, think playing intentional wrong notes is humorous. They should be replaced as soon as possible.

HEADSETS

After all individual balances are taken, play a tutti section to see if everyone can be heard, and ask if there are any problems with headsets, presuming everyone has them on. For quiet cues, there are usually some string players who are not wearing their headsets and the click leakage will be audible in their mics. Those headsets should be turned off before recording, or remind everyone to wear them.

PREPARE THE PERCUSSION

The percussion players should be told in advance which cue will be recorded next since their instrument setups usually require more time than other players. The mixer might even want to place big numbered signs on the various percussion mics so he can easily see who is playing what instrument and which mic they are on. Just before you begin a break time, inform the percussion players which cue is coming after the break so they can allow enough time to get the instruments they need. Although they usually do, be sure the percussion players are keeping track of which cues need parts to be overdubbed (those which they could not play during the recording). This is obviously very important for a later percussion overdub session.

PLAYER LISTS

Every conductor should have in front of him on the podium a list prepared by the contractor of all the players' names on that particular session and their instruments so he may consult them personally instead of saying, "Oboe, bar 11." I save these lists for future reference because, undoubtedly, at some later date I will want to refresh my memory as to who played what on a certain session. Having this list also helps when others ask for player recommendations.

MISTAKES ALONG THE WAY

If a player's mistake occurs in an easily fixed place (one separated by convenient spots to punch-in and -out), do not stop conducting just because you hear a wrong note. Everything else about the performance may be the best yet and the mistake can easily be fixed by re-playing only a small part of the total cue. Unnecessary repetitions of long cues frustrates players and diminishes their playing "edge." The brass, especially, can become overtaxed and start missing high notes when this happens, so be prudent in what you choose to dwell on. Continue conducting a cue while recording until you're told by the mixer to stop, or until the players ask for a pause.

On the other hand, stop immediately if a mistake occurs early on in a cue (often missing a precise downbeat) for it is pointless to continue on. Stop for room noise or bad notes (unless you're just rehearsing) in places that cannot be punched in.

If certain players are having trouble with their part, first ask if the part is written awkwardly and could be changed to make things easier. If the problem persists, don't spend too much time trying to fix it while the entire orchestra is waiting, but have the player tacit for now and do it later as an overdub to save time, or maybe get a different player to overdub it at a later time, and go on to another cue. Remember how valuable each minute is when you have an orchestra waiting. If a piano is out of tune or a gong is not the right one, it's better to leave it out and do it later as an overdub. The rule is never to put anything on tape that will be a problem later on. Things can be overdubbed but not taken out (unless there was sufficient separation of that sound from the orchestra).

It may seem pointless to mention how a conductor should listen closely to the orchestra, but composers who are conducting for the first time may have trouble focusing on the details of the sound because they are thinking about so many things, such as the video screen, turning score pages, and waving the stick, not to mention the overwhelming euphoria of hearing their music with a live orchestra. I still have my moments of mental blackout when I am conducting where I am just basking in the sound of the orchestra and forget to *think*. Hopefully, you will have a trusted listener in the booth to catch things you overlook.

One of the many things you should be listening for, and thinking about, as you are conducting is the coordination of phrasing between different choirs of instruments along with tricky ensemble rhythms. Take the time to rehearse just the instruments in those particular bars until a clean run through occurs. This kind of thing will come back to haunt you forever if it is not fixed. Remember to tune up occasionally also, especially strings, which tend to need tuning more often.

Longer cues should be recorded in sections in order to save time. This simply allows you to concentrate your orchestra's energy per section and is a big boost in the players' morale when they can focus their performance. It can eliminate the need for unnecessary playing of entire cues, especially helpful for the brass if there are lots of high notes.

A Problem in the Booth

This is a phrase heard more so today with the increased use of computers, for frequently the cause of a problem in the booth is a computer crash. If the mixer is not ready to record, for whatever reason, don't just sit and wait, eating up time. First ask how long the problem may take to correct, then do something like:

1. Take a needed break. Even if it's not time for a break, you might be able to take one now and skip the next. Consult your contractor.

2. Rehearse the current cue if need be, or if you are nearly done with it and there is nothing more to say about it, rehearse the upcoming cue, if it is not one that requires a big change of instruments, especially percussion.

3. Tune up.

Perhaps, if you have never thought of yourself as a conductor, you have had no interest in watching them closely to observe their vocabulary of gestures. You might find it is not as complex an ordeal as you imagined to achieve a level of technique enabling you to conduct your own music at a recording session. Ask someone who is conducting a recording session if you can stop by to observe. Maybe attend a symphonic rehearsal to watch the conductor, or pick up a few videos of orchestral performances for study. You will find a wide range of styles from one conductor to another. Some are very flamboyant and others are very economical in their movement. Choose which is best for you, and then try to practice conducting to a recording in front of a mirror and compare your gestures with those of your video. Or, better yet, get a teacher to put you on the right track toward a technique that will enable you to conduct your own scoring sessions. You might be glad you did.

Fix it 7

e assured that film scores are never really finished until the final mix is complete and a deadline forces the final print to be put in a can for copying and distribution. So be prepared for changes up to the very end. Never sleep too soundly with the director's approval of your score until all has been finalized. Even if your mockups bring rousing cheers from all sides, be prepared for changes up to the last minute of recording. Sometimes a producer will show up at the session and override the director; maybe he dislikes a cue and demands changes. Or, last-minute film edits might mean you will get a new cut of the film at the recording session, and will have to make changes on the spot.

But whatever changes you may make, save rewriting the entire cue as the last resort. Try every other modification of the written notes first, simply because rewriting is the most time-consuming fix and one that is sometimes impossible to accomplish in the allotted schedule. Rewriting cues can be done many times *before* the recording sessions begin, but after that, time is taken up with recording, writing any last minute cues, recording overdubs, and beginning the film mixing sessions. So making fixes quickly at a session is something at which you should become very adept.

The following discussion of fixes is intended for composers familiar with conventional musical notation. If you are unfamiliar with it, then obviously, to fix cues at the session you must bring your orchestrator and conductor together for a meeting with the director to see how the director's changes can best be realized. Let's begin with those fixes done while you are still at your computer.

IT DOESN'T WORK

Beginning film composers might be thrown off guard by the rejection of their music by the director. If he simply says, upon seeing the film with your computer mockup, "It doesn't work," what to do then? He can tell you the reasons for his feeling, and you can explain the reasons why you think it does work and then try a rewrite if he is still not convinced. All the while, you must realize that you are not likely speaking to a person who understands your musical perspective and that you will probably have to make a special effort to see the director's view of what the score should be. You are becoming a player in his dramatic process and your every note will have an effect on the feeling of a film that he has been working on for many months, or even years. Some directors are willing for you to take the lead but some are not, and ultimately, it is the director who has the final say.

Your first response to "It doesn't work" should not be a complete rewrite of the cue. If you are at the recording session, there is often not enough time to rewrite the cue. Sometimes the problem can be simple to fix, an orchestral color that is displeasing or an element of motion buried in the strings which, when simplified, can make a huge difference in the dramatic effect.

Almost every director has those instruments that, for some reason, he dislikes. Finding those offenders can sometimes mean an easy solution. Once a student of mine was composing a score for a short film and the director kept saying it was "too beautiful" and should be simplified. So the composer kept taking out notes and still the director said "too big and lush." When I heard it I thought the notes themselves sounded very simple but his particular string patch was very intense and big sounding and I asked if he had tried changing the patch. When he said, "No," I wondered if perhaps that was a simple fix that the director was trying to verbalize but couldn't make clear.

Even the most seasoned composers can have trouble coming up with music that satisfies a director, so don't be too shaken if you have to do five or ten rewrites until you find something the director likes. This is not uncommon, though very trying, and in this situation, patience is your most redeemable virtue.

Eventually you will arrive at mockups that the director approves, and you can send these to your orchestrator to begin score and part preparation for the recording sessions. But be prepared for more changes after you begin recording, as there is always the possibility that even with all the previewing there may be new forces at play that will require changes at the session.

CHANGES AT THE RECORDING SESSION

Quick fixes to your scores at the recording sessions have to be done for many reasons. There could be a new cut of the film arriving as you are recording and timings will change. Sometimes a whole new scene is shot and needs music at the last minute. Or, simply, the "wind could be blowing differently that day," and what was perfect when playing your mockups seems less so now. In any event, don't be surprised about last minute changes. They are simply part of the film business routine.

The following are some possible ways of fixing cues without resorting to complete rewrites. Obviously your mockup was okay thus far, so there must have been a lot that was right about it, and a slight alteration or two should be all that is necessary. Be careful of changing too much in the way of eliminating instruments at the session, because you can then end up with real balance problems. The players can be very flexible in terms of their performance, so it is good to talk through softer dynamics or muting effects before taking instruments out. I've seen miscommunication between the director and composer result in lots of wasted time making changes that were too drastic, only to finally return to the original form because it was "pretty close after all."

THE MUSIC SOUNDS TOO BIG

When a director says he feels your music is too big, that can mean several things. First, the obvious one is that the dynamic is too loud because maybe the entire ten brass are playing forte and in the higher part of their range. The fix is to first try lowering the brass dynamic and maybe lowering some of them an octave, and if that doesn't work, take out all brass except the French horns playing softly. It could be possible that the director feels it is too big even with no brass playing. If the orchestration has a wide spread to the strings and woodwinds, with piano and harp active as well, maybe it is not too loud but rather too full. In this case it could be the number of various lines or parts that add up to a thick sound. The players are capable of playing extremely softly, and if this alone is not sufficient, then you must have some players tacet. Maybe the feeling of big is the result of a few crescendi or sforzando hits that are objectionable, or possibly some cymbal, timpani, or bass drum rolls or hits. Omitting these might be just the ticket.

A lighter articulation could suggest a smaller sound, and that may be appropriate. One thing an orchestra can do extremely well is change its character with instruction from the conductor, "More spiccato strings and sul tasto; brass, not so heavy and sustained but lighter, more playful." These kinds of fixes can be accomplished without any changing of notes, and can make a huge difference in sound.

Thinning the Orchestra

The no-brainer here is to remove the loudest instruments first. The tricky part is to be sure that, if the instruments you take out do not have their lines doubled in other instruments, you must re-orchestrate. Usually, for loud tutti sections, there are some woodwinds or strings doubling the brass an octave above. These higher instruments can be lowered an octave to replace the brass, and the lowest notes can be eliminated or moved up an octave. If not, consider putting the original brass music in piano or synth for a quick fix, otherwise, re-orchestrate and do this cue at a later session. Adding mutes is a good way to thin the brass or string sound because, in both groups, the muting effect actually reduces the number of vibrations emanating from the instruments, thus making the band sound smaller than it normally is. And, of course, most woodwinds can play as quietly as you could ever need.

Example: an originally loud brassy passage might need to be more mellow and subdued, so maybe adding brass mutes would work (if the contractor has told the players to bring them). Or, if the strings were "shadowing" the same brass figures an octave higher, possibly you could tacet the brass altogether and have the strings play quietly an octave lower. Or, if an ethereal kind of lightness is desired, and the strings were playing half or whole notes, you could ask them to play their parts in a comfortable range as harmonics, as long as the notes do not change too quickly.

Example: if a passage is too busy (too much motion), be prepared to tell the players how to simplify their parts, maybe take out the eighth-notes between beats so they play all quarter notes, giving a broader, less busy effect.

First try everything *but* changing notes, and that can often be sufficient for creating a smaller sound.

The Music Sounds Too Small

What if the director feels the music should be bigger? The first thing to try is increasing the dynamics or adding some crescendi or sforzando hits accented by percussion. However, it is not nearly as easy to add parts for a big sound as it is to take them out for a small one. That is why orchestrators try to anticipate having enough notes on the page to work with that will cover the loudest dynamic possible for the scene, which can then be thinned out if necessary. This could be called "scoring defensively," which becomes a natural instinct after you've spent time running around adding notes to players' parts who were originally tacet. This can take lots of time because their parts usually have multimeasure rests and there is no convenient space in which to write new music. To have the copyist prepare new parts, especially for the strings, might be prohibitive for the time you have available.

Example: If a passage needs to be bigger and the important material was in the woodwinds, you could have the copyist print the woodwind parts for your brass section in the appropriate keys and ranges. This should take only ten to fifteen minutes, maybe while the band is on a break.

Following are a few quick fixes that can help fatten the sound of the orchestra without writing too many new notes.

1. Nothing fattens the orchestral sound more than four (or more) French horns playing full chords rather than unisons, open intervals, or octave doublings.

2. Possibly have the entire mid to upper brass section double a line (unison or octaves) instead of just one or two horns or trumpets. It's not always chords that fatten the sound, but also the strength of the line in question.

3. Change any staccato notes to full eighths or quarters, asking for a "more tenuto feel."

4. Consider changing mid to low brass notes to longer durations and possibly adding octaves below the existing bottom notes (maybe for low strings as well).

5. Change an oboe solo to a trumpet solo by asking the copyist for a new trumpet part with the oboe part included and transposed for the right key (often it is simply the quality of the lead instrument(s) that is uncomfortable to a director).

The list goes on, but these examples should get you thinking about possibilities. If you know ahead of time that the director is unsure about the treatment of certain cues that might be big or small, you should prepare a few different versions that can be simply played in succession for comparison. You might want to record multiple versions so the director can choose later which he likes the best.

Occasionally a director will simply say that he does not like something about the cue but doesn't know how to identify what that something is. Again, if it passed your mockup test then chances are the fix is something small. Do not rush to rewrite until you try:

1. Changing the lead instrument, add or tacet octave doublings of a melody.

2. Eliminating any prominent accompaniment (e.g., harp arpeggi, perc ostinati, harpsichord, high violin doublings, or unusual ethnic instruments that may be cutting through the texture).

3. Considering there might be too much motion in the accompaniment (alberti eighth-notes in the violas or piano, or 16ths in a snare drum). Obviously, try adding these if the director asks for more motion.

Everyone has his least favorite instruments, but directors do not always know in advance what theirs are, so you might need to spend a little time experimenting to see what these might be.

QUICKLY FIXING WRONG NOTES

If your players' parts have been proofed by listening to them section by section in the computer, chances are there will be no wrong notes. But if wrong notes exist when you begin rehearsing the band, there are quick ways to identify what and where they are.

When a wrong note occurs within a single instrument's melody line, this is rather apparent and the player will usually take care of it himself by asking the orchestrator or librarian to check the score. If the error is nestled in among an orchestral tutti chord, it could be more problematic to find, especially if the harmony is atonal. To find and fix a wrong chordal note, try the following:

1. Focus on the bar(s) where the wrong note is heard and play the suspected wrong chords one by one as though each were a whole note. If the wrong note is still elusive, do the same thing a section at a time, brass, then woodwinds, then strings. When the fix is made, return again to a tutti and see if the problem is resolved. This is so much faster than simply playing through the passage at tempo over and over hoping to hear it as it flies by. Sometimes, just saying to the orchestra, "There was a wrong note in bar 27" will be enough and an attentive player will say, "It was me, it's okay now." Voila.

2. If you already know that the error was not in the quicker melodic notes, but in the longer accompanying ones, simply ask, "Let's hear the 'long-note' people at bars 27 and 28 very slowly." This will focus attention on where the problem is without the distraction of parts which are okay. Or you can identify the people you want to hear as "the tied-over people in bar 8" or "the staccato people in bar 23," etc. Try any shortcut you can think of with the minimum of talk to save time.

Also, instead of trying to name specific pitches of a tonal chord that needs to be fixed, you might say something like, "The downbeat of bar 7 is C major not C minor, so anyone playing a concert E♭ please make it an E natural." It is not necessary to look at the score and locate every instrument playing a concert E♭ and tell them individually to change to an E natural. Not only is it time-consuming, but very difficult and potentially embarrassing for conducting composers who might not be that quick with instrument transpositions.

There is a story that, with a minimal amount of sessions to record in Prague, a conductor figured he could save time by asking the concertmaster to instruct the musicians to raise their hands if they played a wrong note and he could then quickly fix any errors. The concertmaster, without hesitation, replied this would not be a good idea since the players would abuse the rule by raising their hands frequently just to go into overtime. So much for planning ahead.

It may not seem like such a big deal to take these kinds of shortcuts for a few fixes, but during a three-hour session, the time taken for fixes can be significant. At the end of a final session, you may save enough time to get another take of an important cue. Remember, you only get 50 minutes to record out of every hour because ten minutes of it is break time, so a three-hour session is really only two-and-a-half hours of recording time.

CORRECTING BALANCE BY OVERDUBBING

Sometimes when the budget restricts you to a fairly small string section (10, 8, 6, 4, 2 or fewer) but you have a fairly large brass section for reasons of style, the brass may overshadow the strings and woodwinds and bleed into all mics so much so that the only way to reconcile a balance between the brass and the rest of the orchestra is to record the orchestra playing first without the brass, then overdubbing the brass separately. This allows total control over the volume of the brass in relation to the rest of the band. The downside is that it diminishes a nice blend when all the sound happens at once and each section reinforces the other. Only do this when you have to.

DIALOG

Try as you might to steer clear of stepping on dialog, there are times when a composer may be too involved with the music and forgets to check whether his score is obscuring something important. For this reason, it's always preferable to hear your session playbacks with dialog whenever possible, because only then will you know whether dialog is being covered by the music. The director will never say, "I guess the dialog got covered" and leave it at that. The composer will have his music turned down later in the re-recording mix so the dialog is heard, and this might be regrettable, especially since it could have been caught and fixed at the session.

If you need to make room for dialog, don't panic, you needn't remove all the music, only those instruments that are in the frequency range of the actor's voice. If it is oboe and it's doubled *8va* by violins, simply remove the oboe, and maybe reduce the dynamic for the other instruments. If the brass is too heavy for the dialog, consider playing softer or using mutes; the same with strings. Or, you could employ the "swiss cheese effect," by simply taking out a beat or so of some or all the instruments here and there where appropriate so the dialog can peak through. This can be refreshing for the music to come and go, especially where the scene is quiet and the dialog is essential.

Some other types of quick fixes you might have to make:

Director says:	**Fix it by:**
too much character in music, more neutral	tell strings no vibrato or use mutes. eliminate crescendo or diminuendo. remove a prominent rhythm or even melody, leaving accompaniment. lighten the entire texture.
too "wholesome" sounding	add harmonic dissonance or a more angular melody. make French horns unison or tacit. maybe change to minor mode. tell strings no vibrato (intonation tough if really high). change a sweet lead instrument to one with more "edge."

make less "rigid" sounding

have certain players read notes as though they had no rhythms, just noteheads.

remove regular perc ostinatos.

more tension

add a half step above a chord (in picc above violin, in horn in mid-range)

move basses up or down a half step.

strings ponticello (maybe tremolo also).

add extremely high or low notes.

less tension

remove more dissonant notes or $\frac{1}{2}$ step accompaniment figures.

more string vibrato for warmer sound.

remove extremely high or low notes.

more motion

add busier rhythm in perc or inner strings, ostinato in KB.

quicken pace of harmonic rhythm.

make quarters repeated 8ths or 16ths.

play bars 2x as fast and repeat them.

less motion

make 8ths or 16ths quarters, halves or whole notes.

slow down harmonic rhythm.

remove ostinati.

play $\frac{1}{2}$ as many bars but twice as slowly.

As mentioned elsewhere, the elements of tension and motion are always focal points of attention for musicians and non-musicians alike, whether they are aware of them or not. These factors play such big parts in the dramatic feeling of a film and the perception of just how much or little of each is required can change like the wind from day to day, so be prepared for alternate ways of handling them.

Also, the particular contexts of where the tension and motion occur determine how they are treated. The motion in a slow romantic cue is obviously very different from a feeling of motion in a fast action chase. Tension is also relative to the context. The interval of a perfect 4th can sound like tension in a tonal style or a major triad can sound like tension in a chromatic setting. One thing is certain, directors feel the effects of these elements more than any other, so the composer must be mindful of their use.

USE RHYTHM SECTION FOR QUICK CHANGES

If you have pop or jazz rhythm section players (piano, bass, drums, guitar), you have at your disposal four players who are used to improvising, reading from chord symbols, doing all kinds of extemporaneous things which could be useful in making quick changes at a session. A set drummer does not need a part to accompany a band if he is asked to fill in a certain feel behind them. This one person can transform a rather stately cue into a pop one or add explosive hits on the conductor's cue or by watching the video. If suddenly a pop tune feel is needed, give them a set of chord symbols and talk down the kind of rhythmic feel you want, and you might hear amazing things. There is often no limit to a good rhythm section's creativity, and they love bringing their inventiveness to your rescue. Just do not abuse their talent to the extent that your score is mostly improvisation, or you will have some composing credit issues to deal with.

The funniest improvisation request I ever heard came from a hip-hop composer when he asked two symphonic oboists to improvise snake-charmer fashion while imagining they were undressing a belly dancer. This was not what was happening in the video, but it was the composer's way of describing the kind of music he wanted, and he seemed satisfied with the result. It had to be a memorable moment for the oboists as well.

FIXING DIFFICULT ENSEMBLE RHYTHMS

If certain players are having trouble at a session playing with an ensemble's rhythmic syncopation (as when legit players are trying to play against some concurring jazzy figures coming from another part of the orchestra), it's best to record just the non-syncopated players first as a unit to click, then overdub the trickier syncopated players on top of that. This can make something that is nearly impossible to perform live, possible.

Another approach to fixing tricky ensemble rhythms occurred when we were having a classical brass quintet overdub a baroque brass part on top of a prerecorded pop rhythm section. After many tries of hearing the brass be consistently late in their rhythmic feel, the recording engineer said he would delay the rhythm section parts before they hit the tape. It worked amazingly well, and the final version sounded as if the brass were really "cooking," when in fact they were lagging behind. We didn't have the heart to tell them what really happened.

FIXING SYNC POINTS WITH THE FILM

Whether because of a newly edited film or a director who simply changes his mind as to where a certain climax is to occur in a scene, you may need to do something like the following. On one session, a climax point was moved a couple of seconds later than planned for a 70-piece orchestra. We had to start at the same place but get to bar 21 two beats later than expected (this happens fairly frequently, especially in the jingle business). So our very capable music editor simply chose to make bar 20 a six-four bar instead of four-four and we had the orchestra extend their figures in bar 20 for two beats. The climax then occurred at the right place. When you do this, remember to subtract the number of beats you added somewhere later in the cue, so the total number of beats remains constant.

Obviously, this can work in reverse as well, but that is always a little trickier to make a melodic phrase feel correct with some beats removed, especially when the music before it was strictly $\frac{4}{4}$ with four-bar phrases, but it can be done. Again, if you remove beats, remember to add them later in the cue.

FIXES AFTER THE SESSION

With Pro Tools or Sonic Solutions music editing software, certain fixes can be made after the session is over. You can extend measures, fix an isolated instrument's pitch, change tempi, etc. Often, film composers will write a few large cues and then the music editor will edit them into smaller cues. Then, if there is time, the new smaller cues will be re-recorded with the orchestra, saving a busy composer a lot of writing time. Sometimes it may be the only way possible to complete the amount of music necessary for the score.

Once after the fact, we discovered a repeated wrong harp note that was not audible to us until the session was over and the mix was in progress. It was possible in Sonic Solutions to identify that pitch's particular frequency (no one else in the orchestra was doubling it at the time) and nullify it and then replay the correct note as an overdub, something not possible before this software was available.

Another time, a composer was dissatisfied with the pitch of a choir (mainly a soloist) that was overdubbed on several orchestral tracks. Through Pro Tools, the composer was able to painstakingly fix the pitches of the singers to his liking.

These editing techniques could be helpful if you were overdubbing an ethnic instrument that had a limitation of possible keys it could play in. If the recorded orchestra pitch were electronically changed in the software to the appropriate key for the soloist to play, it could be then taken back to its original key after the soloist's overdub was complete and it would sound as though the ethnic instrument was played in an impossible key.

CONTEMPORARY TECHNIQUES AS COLORISTIC EFFECTS

There are some simply produced techniques from contemporary classical music that can be added easily at a session for dramatic effect. These and many other effects can be found on the first pages of published contemporary scores with their accompanying symbols. Not all sound libraries have these sounds available for you to demo for the director in advance, so they can only be heard live at a recording session. They are included in this chapter because they are changes made to your pre-existing parts at the session. Only if you are sure of approval can they be included with the original orchestration. Since the predictability of the success of these techniques is problematic, you will have to take some time at the session to audition them. You will need to have alternative notes already on the score and in the parts in case the exotic ones are not approved. In any event, if you have time to do a little experimenting, they are well worth trying and have the potential of being an interesting addition to your score. If you are unfamiliar with them, ask an orchestrator for help.
Some of these are:

1. String effects, such as playing on the "wrong side of the bridge," playing each instruments' highest note simultaneously, quarter-tone clusters, harmonic glissandi, ponticello tremolos, portamento (together or in short cascades of individual ones), snapping the string against the fingerboard, etc.

2. Brass and woodwinds blowing air through their instruments but making no pitch, or just the clicking sound of the woodwinds' keys (soft effect).

3. Flute whistle tones (recorded separately because they are very soft) or high forte fluttertongue notes or clusters added at peak moments.

4. Give players four or five pitches to play randomly in different free rhythms.

5. Have the players watch the video and improvise any of the above, on cue from the conductor.

You could take a few minutes before the session to try some of these sounds at random for the director to hear just to get an idea of what to use where. Rehearse just the areas where these effects would be used as a test. I wouldn't take too much time with this, but it might produce some interesting contrast to the rest of your score. If the director likes some of these sounds, you might want to record them "wild" (without click), especially ones that are non-pitched. They could be included later at the mixing session and inserted anywhere you like.

Employing improvised orchestral sounds should probably be attempted only with experienced players who are familiar with them. Have specific techniques in mind (maybe ask players about them before the session for their input), but at the session don't let the experimentation get too involved or you will lose the attention of the players and the director as well. Sparingly used, they can be effective coloristic touches.

FIXING THE FILM

Having said a lot about fixing the music, can the music in turn fix a film? This is something student composers will probably be asked to do when they are working on student films that can be rather roughly cut or seemingly incomplete. And, to a certain degree, a score can sometimes help smooth over rougher parts of a film, give a feeling of breadth to a very choppy one, or give a sectional feel to a film with little contrast. The director may even say that he was not pleased with the edit he has and would like you to help accomplish certain things the film is not doing on its own. So it is a noble try at best, sometimes successful and sometimes not, depending on the amount and scope of fixing required. One thing is sure, the potential influence a score can have on a film is so great, you should not rule anything out until you try it. After all, film music is anything but an exact science.

KEYBOARD®

BUSINESS REPLY MAIL
FIRST-CLASS-MAIL   PERMIT NO 1286   BOULDER CO

POSTAGE WILL BE PAID BY ADDRESSEE

KEYBOARD.
PO BOX 50404
BOULDER CO 80323-0404

Recording

*N*ow let's look at some of the challenges you'll face when working in the recording studio. A general rule of thumb is to book one three-hour session for each seven to ten minutes of score, more or less depending on the difficulty of the music (this includes the usual ten-minute break per hour required under musician union rules). This means a 60-minute score could comfortably be recorded in six to seven sessions, pending any unforeseen major setbacks like computer crashes, rental equipment that either does not arrive on time or doesn't work, construction noise next door—anything that might cost you extra time. Check with your mixer to be sure all is going according to plan and if there are any sessions before or after yours that might squeeze your chances of starting on time or infringe on any overtime option. If you have to lose an hour of recording time out of a single three-hour session to fix a problem, then you will likely not complete your recording. If you lose an hour over six or seven sessions, it is not nearly as critical. The most unpredictable element in the mix is the computer crash. Make sure that the programs used are familiar to the mixer and the studio's resident assistants. It's like asking a doctor before an operation if he has performed this routine before. Check everything possible to avoid delays: players, equipment, rentals, piano tuning, even traffic considerations at the time of your sessions if necessary. There will be plenty to deal with that you cannot predict, so anticipating whatever problems you can foresee puts you that much ahead.

On very luxurious projects, I have seen entire sessions go unused because we completed all cues earlier than expected. There was ample time to listen to playbacks with video, discuss different approaches with the director, retry takes with slight changes, replay the best cues for the director's friends when they show up—there was even time to mix in the same large studio we recorded in.

The opposite can also happen, where your budget is so slim you wonder if you should even be there in the first place. No time for playback of the audio, let alone with video. You finish recording one cue, ask the mixer if he was sure he got it, and immediately go to the next cue. Sometimes we have done up to 20 minutes of score per three-hour session. Another very minimal budget forced me into a situation with the worst studio ever. It was so cheap they asked me if I could loan them money to go out and get some more headsets for the players. They even asked if I brought any two-inch tape with me. In addition, the 24-track machine started running slow, and we were thankful we even got a recording to take with us. It was my fault for not checking out the studio more carefully in advance.

If you are in a low-budget crunch, a smart approach is to keep the synth tracks that sound pretty good as they are and sweeten them with live instruments in the studio, eliminating the cost of replicating the entire score. Overdubbing a pre-existing synth track with a few acoustical instruments is a way of saving money and still maintaining some sense of the live sound.

In general, it is more expedient to record as many players at the same time as possible. On a very big budget film, I witnessed a quartet of piano, bass, drums and guitar recorded separately, in that order. To this day I do not understand why. They were playing pop music, and their interactions and "groove" would have been a plus, in my mind, and a lot cheaper in terms of studio time. But the composer chose this bizarre approach for some unknown reason. The recording sounded okay but rather lifeless. I remember the piano player asking (since he recorded first) whether it was okay to include a certain improvised figure at a certain place and the composer said no because the guitar would be doing something else at that place when he recorded later. Strange.

Recording directly to digital two-track is an option that can save money, obviously eliminating the mixing stage of the process. This can only be done when you have either the option to hear the playbacks yourself, or there is someone you trust in the booth listening for you as you go.

CHOOSING THE RIGHT MIXER

Naturally having someone that you have worked with before is a major plus. But if that is not an option, it would be good to ask around for names of people who have recorded your style of music before. Talk to them about their experience and listen to samples of their work. If you have certain preferences for overall sound that you want to incorporate in this recording, you should play examples of them for the mixer in advance, asking if he is familiar with how to achieve what you want to hear, such as a certain string section quality or "pillowy" room sound, or maybe an old-fashioned Max Steiner sound for a period film. If the studio you are renting says they can include a mixer in their usual price, be sure he is the right person for your style of music. You don't want to hear what can happen when a rock and roll mixer records an orchestral session.

Regardless of the mixer you use, you must give him a list of the instruments you are using for each session in advance and play him some of your mockups so he can get an idea of the style he is dealing with. This can affect all sorts of future decisions, like mic choice, mic placement, and seating arrangement. You can discuss the pros and cons of the whole band wearing headsets or if just the conductor needs them for the click, which is a simpler approach. If the band will have to rely on hearing each other acoustically in the room, placement of instruments is crucial. If piano and celli are doubling some important figures and they are 50 feet apart, you could have some problems in ensemble precision.

You should have at least two room mics placed fifteen feet or so above the front of the orchestra in addition to close mics for each section of strings and separate mics for brass, woodwind, and percussion players. Depending on the rhythmic nature of the music, you can switch back and forth in your mix between close and room mics for the right blend.

Placement of instruments in the studio is important to consider. The mixer usually plans this acoustically, giving the French horns a place in front of a wall to reflect their sound, piano with the lid reflecting sound away from the rest of the band. If the acoustic grand piano is the featured instrument you might want to put it in the center of the orchestra with the lid completely off, so that it's sound will circulate into all of the mics. And if you are recording bagpipes, the best place for them would probably be in the parking lot.

In all, you want a mixer who is "on your side," not one who feels compelled to give you more instructions than you need (unless you want that kind of support). I have been on sessions where the mixer seemed to be in charge and it became more of an obstacle than a help. Ask your prospective mixer if you can visit a session of his and you will see first hand if his working style would be comfortable for you and your style of music.

If you are conducting and don't have time to listen to playbacks yourself, it is wise to have someone whose ears you trust in the booth next to the mixer to guide him through the score as to when certain instrumental solos are coming and the relative quality and volume of some things like cymbals or counterlines or important doublings that can be missed if the mixer himself is not following a score.

Large string sections are sometimes grouped with the second violins to the right of the conductor, rather than next to the first violins. If you have at least fourteen or more first violins, you might want to try this for a "right-left" interaction with the seconds. If you have fewer than fourteen first violins, I feel it is better to have all violins next to each other for mutual support, richness of sound, and intonation.

WHERE TO RECORD

It is important to discuss the best studio for your music with the mixer. There are definitely pros and cons to each recording venue that can vary on a room-to-room basis. A jazz quartet in a room that can fit a 90-piece orchestra with wood floors and walls might not be the ideal sound. By the same token, if you are limited on funds and choose to record a large group section by section in a small studio you will probably lose not only the reverberance of a larger space, but also the natural blend of each group into all the other mics.

In terms of video playback, some very small studios don't have a capability of playing back music with video, and if that is a requirement, you need to get a studio that does. Also, the studio will tell you what their price includes. Sometimes things like the mixer, drum set, Hammond organ, or ProTools are included in the price. If you bring your own, they should give you a discount. One time when the mixing facilities were inadequate at the studio in which we recorded, we said we wanted to go elsewhere for the mix. They refused to give us the master reels until we paid for the entire mixing time, even though we were not using it. So try to ask enough questions going into an agreement that will prevent such catastrophes. In every area of the recording process the rule is always, "ask first, ask first, ask first," whether it concerns the mixer, the studio, the contractor, or the players. Most studios allow cheaper rates for "off hours," so if you don't mind recording very late at night, this might be a way of saving money.

If you are considering recording in Eastern Europe (Prague, Bratislava, Warsaw, etc.), there are some pros and cons. The musicianship of the players there is excellent. However, you might have a problem communicating American pop or jazz figures that seem second nature to us. Be sure you have players who will understand such idioms without a lot of explanation.

THE STUDIO ASSISTANTS

Every mixer will have assistants who do all kinds of things that can go unnoticed. They keep track of the various takes, noting which ones are best and which need overdubs. They attend to mic placement, temperature control, replacement headsets, music stands, lighting, and lunch menus; almost anything you might need in this regard can be handled by them. And they are always so helpful and pleasant to work with; don't hesitate to ask them for help when you need it.

RECORDING ORDER OF CUES

There are at least a couple of approaches to the order in which you choose to record your cues. A few directors will insist that they want to go chronologically through the film from beginning to end. If you explain to them the much more favorable approach of going by instrumental makeup of the sessions, doing all the big cues first, the medium-sized cues next and the smallest ones last, they will usually concede. It is important to start a session with a cue that will set the stage for the mixer in terms of balance and setup, especially with regard to the percussion. You don't want to start with a cue that is so long or difficult that it cannot be finalized within, say, an hour or so. It is frustrating to everyone if progress is not achieved fairly early on. Then, after a few cues of the same style are completed, all will feel a sense that things are progressing. If the first cue takes the entire first session or more, it can be frustrating and counter-productive. The brass can become worn out by an over-abundance of high parts and everyone begins to feel that all of the cues will be as laborious and attention span diminishes, which can influence performance. Be assured that after the first cue is complete, the following ones will proceed much more rapidly.

Cues containing the same thematic treatment can easily be done sequentially. If the next day's orchestra is made up of different players, you will need to rehearse the new people, and time is lost if you are doing cues that are in the first day's style. Check with the contractor to see which players will be returning.

PERCUSSION

While you might think you can save money by having one percussionist play all seven perc parts, you might end up spending more than you would by having seven separate percussionists play live, considering all of the overdubs. Plus, you lose a very important quality of sound in the ensemble performance, especially if there is any kind of "groove" happening between the percussion players. It is always better to have all the players there together if possible. An occasional bass drum hit or cymbal crash is fine for overdubbing, but if there are long sections where many instruments are playing, it is best to hire more players.

Consult with your "lead" percussionist about what instruments they have available in addition to the usual ones listed in the orchestration books. They usually have lots of exotic sounds they would be happy to show you. If you have an unusual sound in mind but can't imagine what instrument to ask for, sing the quality of sound to your main player and chances are he can find an instrument to do just that. Percussionists usually have an amazing wealth of sound possibilities at their disposal and will delight you with more choices than you could ever use. Be sure your percussionists are consulted well in advance of your instrument needs, as they might need time to get them in order. You could also inform them of how many parts you have and ask their opinions about the most efficient ways to record them. If the percussionists don't actually own all of the instruments you may need, they might have access to sampled synth versions of them, which can sound quite good.

OVERDUBBING

The percussion section is usually where the most overdubs occur. Very often, the existing players can cover most of the parts, but there will be that extra bass drum or cymbal part that is not possible. If you foresee a lot of percussion overdubs, you had better schedule extra time accordingly. Sometimes we routinely have an hour after each session just for such things. This can be minimized if the parts given the percussion players are done in a fashion that enables them to see the entire percussion section at a glance; all parts can be grouped on one legal size landscape-oriented part (except timpani, which should be a separate part). These players are amazingly able to cover more than we arrangers think, and by giving them a complete composite of all parts you might not have to do as many overdubs as you thought. (Chapter Nine, Score and Parts, for more on percussion parts).

If the brass is overwhelming the more delicate string and woodwind sections, you might want to overdub the brass separately so that their volume can be controlled. The downside of this is that you lose that wonderful blend of a tutti in all mics.

If you are overdubbing instruments of unchangeable pitch (like accordion, harmonica, ethnic winds, etc.), you should have them record a reference track to which the orchestra can tune before recording.

VOCALS AND SOLO INSTRUMENTS

If a singer is uncomfortable singing live with the orchestra, or does not feel secure enough with their part to do a final take when the orchestra records and it would require too many takes to get them to do a good one, you have three options:

1. Record the singer live with the orchestra in an isolation booth so that you can overdub a new take later if necessary after the orchestra has gone,

2. Record the singer after the orchestra has recorded its parts, or

3. Have the singer record their part first with a "dummy" piano track or synth mockup and have the orchestra follow them in their headsets. The live version is best for all when possible.

Discuss with your mixer the possibility of having separate rooms to isolate vocalists or solo instruments. With any soloist, like vocalist, harp, harmonica, acoustic guitar, etc., a separate room will allow the sound to be controlled individually, whereas they might get lost if they were in the studio with the rest of the orchestra. Certain percussion are also isolated in separate rooms (e.g., drum set) because they are either too loud to control with the overall orchestra sound or because what they are playing might be eliminated later in the mix, like a questionable bowed cymbal, ratchet, or chime part.

Synth Pre-records

One last important item; you should have available to the director all the sounds that will be associated with a particular cue as the orchestra first performs it. This means that if you have any really loud instruments (like bagpipes or bass drum roll) that cannot be recorded when the orchestra plays because of the overwhelming volume, then the synth version of this sound from your mockup should be played along with the live orchestra when they do the first run through. Understandably, directors are not thrilled when told that the sound of the cue in its entirety will be coming at some later date and what they are hearing now is incomplete.

Score and parts

In the days before computers, a copyist would often have some difficulty reading what notes a composer or orchestrator had put on his pencil score. Each had his own "style" of calligraphy, usually ranging from bad to worse, and a copyist frequently had to use his musical intuition just to interpret what were often very difficult scores to read. Today, if a copyist is working from an orchestrator's computer notation files created in Sibelius or Finale, his time is no longer spent in deciphering what pitches to copy, but rather printing scores, extracting parts, and formatting them. Because beginning film composers are usually their own copyists, they need to be familiar with the conventions of music preparation. As budgets increase, they can bring in a professional copyist, but even then, knowledge of professional quality scores and parts will be helpful in evaluating a copyist's work or fixing parts on the spot while conducting.

It cannot be overemphasized how crucial the correct preparation of conductor's scores and players' parts is to the film scoring process. I get the impression from some students that since this part of the process doesn't interest them they can give it minimal attention, not realizing that it will cost them valuable studio time to make fixes, which in turn could mean they will not complete recording their score. All the hard work prior to the recording means nothing if it is not given ample time and care in the studio. So, whether you hand copy or print from a notation program, there are basic minimum requirements that must be met to ensure a good performance.

BASICS
Conductor's score

1. There must be a score for the conductor, even if the composer conducts and feels he knows the music; when questions arise a score will enable him to provide quick answers.

2. The score must show all instruments in standard "score order" from top to bottom (woodwinds, brass, percussion, and strings), with the same instrument layout for each page, even if some staves are empty. No optimized scores for conductors.

3. Each page must be complete; no partial pages that need to be combined or pasted together.

4. All pages must be taped "accordion style," edge-to-edge, so that pages do not get out of order or fall off the podium. Never staple conductor's scores in the top left corner like a term paper.

5. Every page must be numbered and have the title of the cue, instrument names for each stave down the left side and bar numbers clearly legible for each bar, not simply for the first measure.

6. All markings must be legible and not overly crowded with notes or staves. If necessary, photocopy the score onto 11 x 17 paper.

7. If a score is handwritten in pencil, and is sufficiently dark, photocopying will improve the clarity immensely. Pencil marks can smudge, fade or reflect light in strange ways that make reading difficult.

8. Never use repeat signs with first, second, or third endings. Write all the music out, even if repeats are literal, otherwise this can be a source of confusion.

9. The score should also show any synth parts which have been pre-recorded and will not be played live. Also, it may be necessary to have the synth parts available to be played in the players' headsets for tuning or coordination purposes.

Players' parts

1. Never use colored paper, only white or off-white.

2. No more than four bars per line, even fewer if there are many notes.

3. Only violins, violas, or celli can share a part on one music stand. Everyone else must have a separate part. That means, for example, you never have flute and oboe, tuba and cello, or even French horn 1 & 2 sharing the same part.

4. If handwritten in pencil, be sure pencil is dark and photocopy for clarity.

5. Multiple pages must be taped edge-to-edge (accordion style) and never left as separate pages that could get out of order or fall off the stand. And, of course, never staple in the top left-hand corner.

6. Every line must have a clef and key signature at the beginning and bar numbers *beneath* each measure that do not collide with notes. If a part is consistently mid to high range, the bar numbers should be below the staff (and occasionally above for low parts).

7. Parts should be legible from a few feet away, so allow space for notes to be large enough to be easily read.

8. Never use repeat signs with first, second, or third endings. Also, do not have first and second endings of a repeated section in one part and the music written out in another as this could cause a discrepancy in bar numbers or simply confusion if a question arises. Better yet, have *no* repeat signs for anyone.

9. Avoid accidental clutter by using sharps for ascending notes and flats for descending ones.

10. Always use multi-measure rests rather than a series of single empty bars, and group them by 8's or less (i.e. do not show a large number of rested bars by a single large number, like "23," but rather 8-8-7, or according to the phrase structure).

11. All players should have the same layout with respect to the form of the music. For example, if the third beat of bar 21 has a fermata, all players should see that clearly, even if they are not playing at that moment.

12. Show any questionable parts to the players *before* the recording session so you will have time to make any changes they may suggest. Waiting until the session has started is asking for trouble.

13. Do not try to conserve paper. Use as much as necessary to produce clear parts that are graphically pleasing, not threatening.

14. New sections should begin on a new line.

15. Never cramp notes onto one line to avoid an additional page.

16. Lines and pages should end with rested bars when possible. Plan ahead for those times when a player has to turn a page and make sure there is ample time to do it without making noise.

17. Dynamics are uniform in size and position below the staff.

18. Single (✗) or double (✗✗) measure repeat signs should used for many repeated bars in a row, especially in percussion parts. MIDI files do not use repeat signs so they must be added to the parts in a notation program.

Take the opportunity to look at some parts done by a professional copyist who frequently works on recording sessions (classical parts for orchestras can look very different). Remember, a recording session is a sight-reading event, and the clearer the parts, the more smoothly your recording session will be.

PRINTING THE SCORE

If there are 20 or more staves on a score, it is usually best to format them for legal size paper, 8.5 x 14 inches, rather than the default letter size of 8.5 x 11. Legal size is standard for all printers and copiers, and the paper trays are readily available. To print a 30 line score on 8.5 x 11 paper simply is not going to work, so don't force it. The staves become too small to read comfortably, and when made larger, the notes, dynamics, slurs, etc. from adjacent staves collide. Another important advantage of legal size score formats, once you print the scores on 8.5 x 14 paper, is that they can be easily enlarged to 11 x 17 for the conductor's score, since the proportions of length to width remain very nearly the same and the score page is filled, eliminating the wasted white space that you get enlarging letter-size paper. I remember one project requesting 11 x 17 scores for the conductor. I was surprised and half-amused when the copyist showed up with the larger paper but the printed area was still 8.5 x 14, which made the larger paper totally unnecessary, except for writing notes in very big margins.

The major computer notation programs offer an option called "optimizing," whereby you see only those staves that contain notes, and empty ones are eliminated. This means some systems may have 20 staves and others three, some pages may have four systems, others one. This is fine for archiving or study purposes, or when you're looking to conserve paper, but never, ever for a conductor. He needs to see all instruments all the time; even when they are doing nothing, blank staves are as important as full ones. A consistent number of staves on each page makes the reading much easier, which in the long run is a time-saver.

Also to be avoided at all costs are scores that have been printed from the notation screen of a sequencer program, where measures without notes sometimes do not even show staves, but simply blank space. It certainly gives a very contemporary look to a score to see staves appearing and disappearing as the eye moves across the page, but it is nearly impossible to read, especially when it is also optimized. Use notation programs for notation and sequencer programs for sequencing. The printouts from sequencer programs are not capable of producing professional-quality scores and parts, so just ignore the blurb on the software box that says they can. The industry-standard notation programs today are Sibelius and Finale, the first being much easier to use.

While it may simplify the extracting of parts in a notation program if each instrument has its own stave on the score, the score will become cumbersome if the orchestra is large (twelve woodwinds, four trumpets, four horns, etc.). As with conventional classical score layouts, you can put two or three instruments on one line of a computer score, stems up and stems down (e.g., two or three trumpets or flutes on a single stave) but *never* in the parts. The players are used to seeing just their part and not multiple lines from which they have to figure out which is theirs. If you try to cut corners here you will definitely pay the price for the time saved formatting and printing with time spent in the studio fixing parts. Each woodwind and brass player must have his own part, as should contrabasses. Violins, violas, and celli have two players on one part and share a music stand. The copyist is accustomed to separating out the instruments into single parts for the players, so create a conventional-looking, easy-to-read score for the conductor with some instruments sharing lines if you wish, and let the copyist do the rest.

It helps a conductor's eye if sectional beginnings start on a new score page. If your music is basically in four-bar phrases, that should be reflected in the layout of the score, i.e., groupings per page of four, six, or eight bars, depending on how busy the music is. It is a little uncomfortable for the conductor to see a major section start on the last bar before a page turn or to see five bars per score page when the music is clearly in four-bar phrases

CHORD SYMBOLS

It is always a good idea to include chord symbols above the piano, guitar, and rhythm bass lines when applicable. It is another way of being prepared for any event that may arise. The recording session does not exist only to document the score as written. It is a fluid process, a work in progress, and chord symbols can sometimes save the day when you have to create music on the spot and you turn to the rhythm section for help. Some guitar players are lost without chord symbols, but few will admit it. The same is true of some jazz/pop bass and keyboard players, so make everyone's life easier (except the drummer's) and give them all chord symbols, or have your orchestrator add them. Do not, however, expect the copyist to do it. Many of them could do it well, but then again, some would not, so it's better to play it safe unless you know for sure.

TRANSPOSED VS. CONCERT SCORES

Scores can be written in one of two ways: In "C" (concert) or transposed, depending on the composer's preference. Actually, with the simple transposition function of notation software they can be written in *two* of two ways, in concert for some (usually the composer) and transposed for others (possibly the conductor or any other legit, non-playing musicians present who may need a score).

To review the differences, transposed scores show each instrument exactly as it appears on the players' parts with respect to their particular key signatures. You will notice on these scores how most of the music lies neatly within or near the staves, with few ledger lines.

Concert scores, on the other hand, will either have many ledger lines or frequent changes from one clef to another in an effort to show the actual pitches of where an instrument is sounding. This can mean that for some instruments, the score can look very different from the player's part (e.g., a bass clarinet or bari sax part, which sound in bass clef but are conventionally written in treble clef when transposed).

For composers new to orchestration, it is potentially confusing that even non-transposed scores will show certain instruments transposed (such as contrabass, piccolo, guitar, etc.) because to do otherwise would result in a veritable plethora of ledger lines, since they sound an octave above or below their actual pitches.

Though I mentioned it earlier in the Orchestration chapter, it is worth repeating that viola should always be written in alto clef on both "C" and transposed scores, period; no treble clef, and no excuses. That is the language of the viola. If a five-year-old Suzuki student can learn alto clef, so can you.

METER AND KEY SIGNATURES

Key and meter signature changes should be kept to a minimum. If a changing-meter section of a score is short-lived and can be accomplished with accents in a more basic meter like $\frac{3}{4}$ or $\frac{4}{4}$, it should be done. Also, frequent key signature changes have proven to be more problematic for sight-readers than the simple indication of the accidentals for chromatic notes over several bars. There is no hard and fast rule, but use your discretion and include key signature changes only for major sections, and do not consider them for transitional moments of two to eight bars or so. Most classically trained composers will think this is ludicrous and an unnecessary dumbing-down of the score, but you must remember that the overriding factor here is not what is intellectually satisfying to see on the page, but rather what will produce the most error-free performance. Surely, if there is ample rehearsal time, you can notate however you would like. But in a sight-reading environment like an expensive recording session, the primary intent is to avoid anything that could cause even the smallest confusion or delay, because, over time, these delays will add up to significant amounts of time and money.

ACCIDENTALS

When working with MIDI file transfers from the composer, there can be a very confusing array of accidentals, often making no sense in the context of any one key signature. This is through no fault of the composer; it's just a MIDI peculiarity if no key signature was included in the MIDI file, which is often the case. This should be cleaned up by the orchestrator or the copyist preparing the parts. In general, ascending notes receive a sharp and descending ones a flat. Notation programs don't always fix this automatically, but it is a major improvement in the ease of sight-reading a part if these are resolved before the session. Imagine yourself reading the part and notate it the way you would like to see it if you were the player. A simple example: when writing the ascending notes C to D-flat to D-natural, a C-sharp in place of the D-flat would make the D-natural unnecessary. Any fixes like this to make the part less cluttered for the player will, in the long run, eliminate time wasted in fixing parts or doing another take after the player has figured out what the part means.

PROOFING PARTS

Proofreading of parts used to be a rather laborious part of the music prep stage, and, if time was really short, it might not have been done at all, sometimes causing nerve-wracking note fixes at the session if the original scores were illegible to the copyist. Today, it is very easy for the orchestrator to play scores on the computer to at least check notes, thus eliminating the need for the copyist to do this. The value cannot be overstated. If there are a lot of wrong notes to fix, it not only costs time, but it can put a real negative spin on the players' morale.

It is one thing to go about fixing wrong notes when the conductor has the orchestrator's handwritten score in front him to use for reference—it is probably correct and the parts were incorrectly copied. However, with computer-notated scores, the parts are printed from the score, and if the players have mistakes, so will the score. You are then trying to fix wrong parts from a wrong score.

PDF SCORES

It is very handy to be able to convert your scores (or parts) into Adobe Acrobat PDF format so you can send them to various exotic places where they might not have your notation program for viewing. You can even send them to your mother, since almost every computer now has the program Acrobat Reader and anyone can see what you're "up to." I've used this more times than I would have thought, sometimes sending scores to producers in Nova Scotia or to secretaries in London who print them out with only the usual office computer. It can save you hours of precious time where otherwise you would have to print everything first and then FedEx all of it.

COPIES OF SCORES FOR THE SESSION

A short but important reminder: Multiple copies of all scores (in their small format of 8.5 x 14 inches) should be made available to everyone who may need them for reference during the recording—that is, the orchestrator, music editor, mixer, etc. The conductor, of course, will have the enlarged 11 x 17 prints (taped edge to edge in accordion style) but everyone else usually prefers the smaller size since they do not have much space in the booth to spread them out.

In fact, if each set of the small scores can be assembled into loose-leaf binders, it makes for easy access, or they can be stapled in the top left corner; the accordion fold is not necessary here as it is for the conductor's scores.

If you come from a classical background you are probably familiar with study scores or even orchestra parts that try to conserve paper and often squeeze as many notes as possible onto a page. The exact opposite is true with recording session scores and parts. Saving paper should *never* be a concern. Making a part or score as instantly readable as possible is paramount, which usually means allowing ample space to spread things out.

If a part is particularly difficult or written for an unusual instrument (like ocarinas or recorders), it is a good idea to send the player the part in advance to work out any problems that would cost you time to fix at the session. Then if the player can offer you some suggestions on how to make the part easier to read you have time to fix it. Letting it go until you are at the session is a risky approach.

PERCUSSION PARTS

As with scores, the legal-size page format can be a really smart time-saving option to use for parts when there is a logistical reason to show as much music as possible on a page (particularly for percussionists, pianists, or harpists). This can reduce the number of pages a player has to turn by as much as half.

Percussion parts in particular can benefit by having all the players see all the parts for one cue (printed in landscape orientation, 8.5 x 14 legal size, with the names of the instruments clearly marked on each stave). This way the players can work out among themselves the best way to cover as many parts as possible when there are numerous lines to record. This format allows them to have the entire cue for all perc in only a few pages. And they'll love you for it. But remember, percussionists are generally farther from their parts than other players, so don't make the notes too small. The default staff size in Sibelius is .28, and this works well most of the time. It can be reduced to .25 or so for piano parts, but never much less than that. Also, piano or harp parts can often be reduced from having four page turns to only a couple by using the legal size paper in the regular portrait orientation, and again, don't make their notes too small. Expect that these instruments normally have more pages than the others, but this is not the time to be saving money on paper.

Assuming your scores originate as MIDI files from a sequencer program, you will often see repeated measures full of notes, since MIDI sequencers don't play repeat signs. For this reason, repeated patterns occurring in percussion parts should have the initial one- or two-bar pattern written at the beginning of a line, followed by repeated measure signs and grouped into usually eight bars per line (or per phrase). This makes sight-reading much easier for the player and will allow for a relaxed performance if they don't have to read notes in every single bar. That becomes tiring over time and only increases the margin of error.

Multiple percussion instruments that can be played by one player (e.g., bass drum and gong, or triangle and woodblock, etc.) can be placed on one staff with stems up for one instrument and stems down for the other, clearly labeling which is which. This will streamline the score and parts by minimizing the number of staves and reduce the number of overdubs necessary later on. If your bass drum is separated from the gong by several staves, it will be difficult for the player to read both at the same time. So take the time to condense the percussion as much as possible.

Symphonic timpanists normally do not play anything but timpani, but on recording sessions this is not true. There is usually a timpani "specialist" who will cover your timp parts but will also play other things if he is free. Just don't expect him to go to and from the timpani very quickly, considering tuning adjustments he may have to make. Avoid the temptation to write a lot of notes for timpani, because if you do, their effectiveness is diminished. Timpani are best used for accenting or rolling (often with a crescendo) and are traditionally written with no key signatures.

Also, because percussionists have to move around, they should have enough multiple copies of their parts so they don't have to carry them with them from instrument to instrument as they move around the section.

Bowings and Slurs

String bowings are, for recording situations at least, best left out, the use of the word "legato" is sufficient, along with a beginning dynamic mark. Put in bowings only where critical for a tutti phrasing. Otherwise, the players actually prefer no bowing marks, because they will invariably change them anyway as per the concertmaster's direction.

As for slurs in the woodwinds and brass, the same is generally true, marking articulation where it is a tutti consideration, but for general legato playing, the word alone is fine. I have found that for very long phrases it is better to simply write all the notes you wish and let the player decide when to breathe, because chances are he can sustain a breath for a longer time than you would expect. If there are players doubling a part, they can stagger their breathing so as not to reveal any breaks in a line. You can note "breathe at your discretion" or "stagger breath" where you want them to sound continuous over an unusually long phrase.

CHANGING INSTRUMENTS

When a player has to make a change from one instrument to another, be sure you allow enough time in the part for him to do it, usually at least two or three bars (e.g., oboe to English horn, Harmon mute to "open," snare drum to marimba, string mutes from on to off, etc.), otherwise you will have to do an overdub, which will cost you valuable time. Consider also if the change could be cause for noise (especially large woodwinds).

HARP

Parts for harp are unlike any other in the orchestra, and you should familiarize yourself with the kinds of parts harpists play. Maybe your copyist has some harp parts from a previous session that you could look at. The unusual look of these parts is a function of their pedal mechanism that allows them only two changes at any one time (one for each foot), and multiple changes are not quickly maneuvered. Each diatonic note can have one of three pedal positions: down, middle, and up (for a sharp, natural, or flat). Because of this, extremely chromatic passages have to be very carefully considered to allow for pedal changes, or a second harp might be needed. If you have questions about your harp parts, consult the player ahead of time.

In conclusion, to learn the best method of producing parts there is no better way than to talk with the players at the recording session on a break about their part. Ask them if it has been written the best way possible or if they would have suggestions about the notation. Players are always more than ready to inform you how to best notate their music. You can learn from their comments about the playability of their part, register, too many notes, or impossible things (e.g., a fortissimo stopped horn or fast harp pedal changes). A clarinet player may suggest eliminating his doubling of an oboe for intonation reasons in a slow melody, or if two instruments are doubling a tricky rhythm, it might be clearer if just one were playing.

The John Williams scores published by Hal Leonard could be helpful in seeing how various instruments of a film score are notated, with all manner of articulation, phrasing, dynamics, etc. Of course, looking at classical scores is always valuable if you wish to learn more about notation; and, over time, you will notice not only discrepancies and similarities but begin to develop a sense of conventional and unconventional models.

Practice

*I*f you are a composer who wants to try your hand at film scoring, how can you practice if you have no films without music? It is not as easy as going to Amazon.com to order them, but finding films with no music is possible.

FILM SCHOOLS

One place to look for films would be a school that either has film scoring classes or filmmaking classes for future directors, screenwriters, and actors. Look on their bulletin boards for infomation on who is looking for composers. Student films are generally short (five to fifteen minutes), and some are very good, but because they are so short, there is little time to practice developing themes or for even having time to employ more than a couple of themes. As you would expect, they can be works in progress that never get completed because of lack of funds, or they can simply look unprofessional. The actors are often students, and the editing work can be amateurish. All of this aside, it can be beneficial to score these projects, which are, in some ways, more difficult than professionally made films. The composer might be in the position of trying to smooth over bad edits or poorly acted scenes, connecting a thread of music across several scenes to tighten a loosely drawn dramatic focus, or bringing back a theme in a way that delineates sections and gives more of a structure to the piece by reiterating musical gestures. You also start to meet director-type people and begin learning a most crucial element of film scoring: how to communicate with a director, who in turn learns from you about the scoring process.

The school may also have a collection of small films without music for their composers to score. Either take a course to get access to these or ask the person in charge if you could get copies of some of them to use for practice.

ANIMATION

Perhaps the film school has filmmakers who do animation as well. This is very different from conventional dramatic films because the music will often be completed first and the animation created around it. What's not to like about that? If the film school does not have animators, and you are near a big city, there are animation festivals just like film festivals where you can meet these very creative people. Some will be working on political statements through their work while others may be doing more entertainment or commercial-type films, so you will find a large range of projects here. Again, these films are generally short because the animators may not have the funds for more than ten- to 20-minute pieces, but often their work is very professional and well worth your while. Because they don't usually hire composers and instead use some form of canned music, you may make no money, at least until they sell their work for professional use, at which time their temp score can be replaced. In any event, they are an interesting bunch to work with as you practice your skills.

FRIENDS IN THE BUSINESS

If you have any friends in the film business (composers, orchestrators, music editors, directors, or producers), they might have working prints of films before the music is added. Maybe they could give you a copy of one or more of these to practice on. The advantage here is that, not only do you have a chance to write a score to a film with no music, you can probably see what was done for their final score as well, to use for comparison. Even if you haven't met them, you might try contacting those who might be able to loan you some materials. Be willing to sign a non-disclosure statement or some form of release, as concerns about piracy these days are very real.

FEATURES WITH NO MUSIC

There are a number of well-known films that have no music and are commercially available on DVD or VHS. Sidney Lumet is a director who has done several films with no music at all *(Dog Day Afternoon, The Hill,* and *Network)* and others with only ten to fifteen minutes of score *(Serpico* and *Long Day's Journey Into Night).* Alfred Hitchcock's *The Birds* is another famous film without a score. True, you are working here with dramatic content that is so intense that music might be in the way, but they are professionally made and are long enough to give you practice thinking about the reuse of several themes over the course of an entire film.

Walt Disney's famous *Fantasia* and the French film *Red Balloon* have scores that you can replace with your own score and not worry about stepping on dialog since there is none. The latter is 30 minutes long and allows you complete freedom to work in a larger but not huge time frame. Also, the beginning of *Butch Cassidy and The Sundance Kid* has a long stretch without music if you'd like trying your hand at a western.

SMPTE TIMECODE

The acronym stands for The Society of Motion Picture and Television Engineers and refers to a series of digital audio pulses, used for timing, that can be burned onto your videotapes. You must have the audio form of SMPTE code on the tape to lock your VCR to the computer sequencer. There is also a visual SMPTE code that can be put on the VHS tape showing elapsed hours, minutes, seconds, and video frames. If you digitize the video, you will not have to worry about lockup, since it occurs automatically once the file is loaded into your sequencer.

DIGITIZING VIDEO

There are conversion boxes (such as Dazzle, or you can even use a digital video camera) through which you can play a VHS tape and convert it into digital video. These files can be stored on a computer, played with a standard QuickTime player, and imported into a sequencer program like Digital Performer or Logic. The locking to film is done internally with no need for SMPTE code (although you can still reference SMPTE numbers in the sequencer as they are part of most sequencer programs in one of several standard elapsed time formats). I am told that it takes at least fourteen gigabytes of hard drive memory to store one hour of VHS video, which sounds like a lot, but not when you consider that, as of today, you can purchase 160 gigabytes of hard drive memory for $200. The popularity of VHS tape is already waning compared to the DVD format. Soon VHS tape will be obsolete, at which time there will hopefully be an easy conversion from DVD to QuickTime.

MAKING YOUR OWN DIGITAL VIDEO

There is always the possibility of acquiring a digital video camera and videotaping a play or a real life sequence of a bus ride around town, a visit to an art gallery, etc., to use for writing a film score. Maybe you have a friend who likes to shoot video and could give you copies of some of his work. Granted, it's a long way from Hollywood, but at least you could become familiar with the process if not working on a real film. This could also give you a demo to play for a professional filmmaker when the opportunity arises. Even though this may sound like a trivial pursuit, you may discover a clever and skillful way to write a score that could reveal a film scoring talent. I have heard that the Coen brothers started making movies on a little Hi-8 video camera and borrowed a VHS recorder on which to copy their edits. Whatever your situation, there are ways of practicing film scoring, but it will take some effort on your part to seek them out.

EDITING PRE-EXISTING FEATURE FILMS FOR SCORING

You can, with some simple video/audio edits made in a program like iMovie, create your own film clips without music for you to practice scoring with original music. Almost every feature film has some moments where there is no music but where scoring could possibly work. Or, places where there is music which could be deleted or replaced if it does not take out important dialog or sound. Since video editing programs like iMovie allow you to extract the audio into a separate track, it can be manipulated independently of the video, which means you can:

1. delete audio (all or in part)

2. move audio to another place

3. copy audio from one section to use as a replacement in another

4. import audio from any other sources

For example, a scene shows a guy on a horse slowly walking down a busy street with the sounds of people talking and horse steps. Suddenly, when he notices a beautiful girl and starts following her, background music begins (but still no dialog). I made this into a scene for scoring by:

1. digitizing the scene from a VHS tape into iMovie

2. extracting a separate audio track

3. deleting the section of audio where there was music but no dialog

4. copying audio from the beginning where there was just street noise as many times as necessary to fill the "audio hole" I had created by removing music

I then had an entire scene with only street noise over which I could add my original music.

The biggest problem with this technique is where there is both important dialog and score together. You could possibility eliminate all sound and re-record the dialog yourself. If the dialog is not crucial to plot or flow of the scene, those moments with dialog can be deleted.

This process is an endless source of film clips for composers to practice scoring. It takes very little video editing ability to accomplish, and it is fun. You will be amazed by how much you can do to alter a film to make it "scoring friendly."

Study

*E*ach new orchestral recording session brings a feeling of anticipation that I am going to learn something I didn't know before, because it always happens. In addition, I am thrilled that, yet again, the sound of the orchestra is being acknowledged as the best medium to communicate the film composer's musical ideas and that the audience will have another chance to hear music created in a way that may be unfamiliar to many of them.

RECORDING SESSION AS A LEARNING EXPERIENCE

Because orchestral sessions are relatively few and far between, and are extremely expensive, every opportunity to experience one should be considered a rare treat indeed. If you are not conducting, take the opportunity to walk among the musicians while they are rehearsing (not recording, since it might be distracting or cause some room noise). This is a rare chance to hear the orchestral sound close up, and the experience will probably be forever burned on your memory. As you walk, have a score with you to follow for your own questions, as well as to give players or the conductor answers to questions that may arise.

If you hear the English horn when you are close to it, can you still hear it as you walk away? How different is the sound as you walk behind the French horns compared to in front of them? You will miss any sounds that are either pre-recorded or are played by instruments in isolation, but you will hear them when, after the rehearsing is done, you go into the booth and hear the playback. Sometimes there is a huge difference, sometimes little. When you get into the booth, can you still hear the woodwinds? Do the strings take on a more balanced role in the booth than in the studio itself?

As I have walked through the orchestra, occasionally a player will say to me that a certain figure could be done differently to enhance the playing or sound (like upbows on the contrabasses for a stronger attack near the frog of the bow, or a question about a conflict in phrasing that will bring about a clearer tutti). I relish these moments to learn more about the player's perspective. I try to remember all of these comments for making my next score even better.

In short, if you leave any recording session no smarter than when you entered, it is only because you weren't listening closely. There are always new things to learn, and the best and most lasting way to learn is by hearing them first-hand at a session. As some educators say, "We want to give students those 'Aha' moments," when something hits you with no explanation but through sheer experience. This can happen if you listen closely.

THINGS TO TEST AT A RECORDING SESSION

As an orchestrator, I like to try new things at every session, as that is the best way to really convince myself of the value of the choices I make. I am always ready to change my experiment if it doesn't work, but either way, I've learned something.

If you are uncertain about the sound of some parts of your score, take a few moments before rehearsing a cue to test your questions. You may be unsure whether to use mutes for brass or strings, whether the strings should play harmonics or normal notes 8vb, or whether you want piccolo or flute. Try just those measures in question first one way, then the other. It does not take much time and you will learn a lot from this to benefit future scores. Don't guess what to write and then feel you have to live with it. The recording session is not a rigid documentation of a score but a fluid process where things can change. If you are at a loss for experiments, you might want to listen closely to:

1. bass trombone and tuba doubling in unison, then in octaves.

2. clarinet and oboe doubling a slow melodic phrase.

3. high-register bass clarinet, which could be played on the usual B♭ clarinet (same with bassoon and contrabassoon).

4. which instruments can best accomplish the term "niente—cresc" (coming out of nothing to a point where they eventually become audible); clarinets are especially good at this.

5. bowed percussion instruments (like cymbals, gongs, vibes, etc.).

6. which woodwind/brass doubles are most effective (i.e., oboe doubled with trumpet, with or without harmon mute).

7. string effects (sul tasto, light harmonic glissandi, the highest note, playing on the "wrong" side of the bridge, etc.)

8. 1st violins and 1st trumpet unison.

I am not suggesting that all or any of the above are necessarily good orchestration techniques, but you should know what they sound like because these kinds of choices will recur as you orchestrate. The list of experiments is endless once you get started. You might already be familiar with the above sounds from the many classical scores you have followed with CDs. But you will never know everything, so let your imagination wander and experiment when you can, always having an alternate fix in mind in case what you thought would happen doesn't meet your expectation.

WHAT TO DO IF YOU HAVE NO ACCESS TO BIG SESSIONS

Students e-mail me with questions about how to get started in the film scoring business when they do not live in Los Angeles or New York. My answer is to begin listening to classical CDs (simpler ones like Haydn symphonies) *with* the scores. Begin with just the first 20 bars or so, and repeat this passage many times until you have noticed what each instrument is doing, its range, the style of part it is playing, and most importantly, the sound of the instrument in its different registers. Eventually you will get to the point where you can look at a certain stave of the score and hear in "your mind's ear" what it will sound like.

There will be some things that you see on the score but do not hear until the instrument arrives at a certain part of its range to begin to peek through the orchestra. Also, by osmosis, you will be experiencing first hand all the other elements of music, phrase structure, instrumental doublings, harmonic rhythm, tonal center shifts, modulation techniques, fluidity of form, and so on. You will have questions as to why this or that is so. For this reason, it is good to listen with a friend or a class where a discussion can ensue about the reasons a composer chose to do something a certain way. This questioning can be a lifelong source of joy to those who like to watch and listen to scores.

As you get more advanced in your ability to follow and appreciate the score-reading process, you will discover such delicacies as scores by Ravel, who, as one of the finest orchestrators ever, will show you how delicately color can be achieved through elements that are not always audible on first listening. After you see the score, you will then begin to hear what it is you are looking at. The score will guide your ear.

Ultimately, you will be able to simply look at an unfamiliar score and know what it will sound like *without* hearing the CD. This is helpful in so many ways, for your conducting as well as your study of composition and orchestration. You learn to look first at the brass section, their dynamic mark and register, to see if their parts will be in the forefront of the orchestra or as background, and to see if the register of the woodwinds will make them prominent or subdued. This may then lead to your ability to compose without the need for a sequencer program to tell you what you have created. It is liberating to get away from the electronics and experience the sound first in your head and then quickly notate it for later entry into the computer.

When I am asked to orchestrate a film in a city away from home, I like to take only pencil and score paper, rather than reecreating my usual computer notation setup, as a way of keeping in touch with the way I began to write scores many years ago. It sharpens my ears to write away from the computer, though it often makes me frustrated at the excruciating expense of time some things take compared to orchestrating the same music at the computer. But I feel it is beneficial nevertheless, and it makes me appreciate the computer approach also, which can seem more remote than working with a pencil and paper at an acoustic piano.

The main value of score study is to become familiar with the manner in which live instruments play most effectively. I have seen some new composers become so influenced by the sounds of their synth patches that they come to expect the same sound from live instruments. One young composer repeatedly asked a very accomplished string section to play with no volume fluctuation whatsoever, ignoring their natural tendency to shape the entrances and conclusions of phrases, no doubt because of a string synth sound embedded in his mind's ear. We must remind ourselves that the computer is just another tool, like the pencil, for arriving at our finished score. The moment of truth is always in the live performance, so let your mind take the lead in discovering new possibilities, and be careful of being limited by your sound modules. If you are emulating live instruments, the goal should be to let those instruments speak naturally and not expect them to sound like your synth, otherwise there is no point in having the live band.

In your score study and listening, if you encounter classical scores with musical terms or instrument names you don't recognize, do not proceed until you find meanings for them. For example, if you guess that the Italian word "tromba" is a trombone or that "timbales" in a Ravel score are the same small Latin drums used by Tito Puente, you will be very mistaken. It is important to be aware of not only instrument names, but expression marks as well; keep a music dictionary close at hand. True, this can take time initially, but as you learn it will go faster. And remember, even if a single page of score takes three days to fully understand, that is far better than speeding through twelve full scores and not understanding what you are seeing or hearing.

As you progress through your score study, to the extent you read about the composer and his musical context in history, you will begin to accumulate a knowledge of period and style, which could be helpful for a film composer when asked to do a period piece. Through listening to a range of composers, you will become familiar not only with musical style and idioms, but the varieties of harmonic language that have been employed throughout history. It may diminish your thrill of feeling you invented a certain musical style that in fact existed in the Middle Ages, but you will be rewarded by having many new possibilities opened to you.

Then, when the moment comes to create your own score, you need not even think consciously about your style. You will forget, for the moment, all you have learned and concentrate on the film and how to best represent it musically. After all, it is the unconscious part of your writing that is your own style based on your particular instincts; the conscious part is technique that you have accumulated over years of experience and call into action as the need arises.

STUDYING FILM SCORES

Studying classical scores and CDs is the easy part. Because most film music does not have a printed score available for study, you now have a real test with only your eyes and ears to guide you. Your experience identifying what you hear (an oboe) with where on the staff it is playing (what its part would look like) will become even more important. As you listen and watch a video, have a pitch reference available (keyboard) to occasionally check where important instruments are playing. When a big brass crescendo ends with an intense high trumpet, locate that note for future reference, as it can often determine the key of an entire cue. Check string ranges, low and high, so you can imagine the registers that the music is occupying, if not the actual notes. Are there string mutes? Do you know what that sound is like?

As an orchestrator, I occasionally get calls from composers who ask me to listen to certain passages from CDs that they would like to emulate in terms of orchestration—what instruments are playing and how a certain sound is achieved. A composer even asked me, after he created a synth MIDI sequence, how I would create the sound we were hearing. He knew the names of the synth sounds he had used to create the sequence (one was indigenous to synths, very electronic), but he was aware of the fact that the name on the patch did not equate with the sound of real instruments, so we had to find the live musical equivalents. Your ability to identify what you are hearing can not only enhance your enjoyment of a score, it could well help you in emulating sounds that you find useful in your own scores. Emulation is a great way to learn; just be careful when it comes to melodies.

As you aurally study film scores you will no doubt notice certain common "filmic musical gestures" (clichés) that reappear in many films; the high string note to subtly introduce a feeling of suspended motion and anticipation, or the low string note for a foreboding ominous effect. Try as you will, it is sometimes difficult to avoid using these conventions, and so be it. If they have worked so often for so many scores, there is probably good reason for it. Don't feel you have to avoid them simply because they were used before. This is film music, and musical gestures are often repeated from score to score. And you can be sure every audience recognizes the rather standard vocabulary of musical clichés that have developed over the years. You may tire of them, and you may want to invent new ones, but in the meantime, you need to be very aware of these clichés and the dramatic weight they possess, using or avoiding them as the situation requires.

TENSION AND MOTION

Because these two musical elements are so crucial to dramatic music, as you study film scores you would do well to track just these elements to see how they are used. Motion is usually connected to the rhythmic pulse and its subdivisions, often defined in the percussion or in parts with a degree of faster rhythm than the rest of the orchestra (eighth notes churning in the violas or a soft snare drum in sixteenths). Or, a sense of forward motion could also be realized from a harmonic progression that can give a tremendous forward pull (such as in Wagner's *Prelude to Tristan and Isolde*). Tension, on the other hand, is commonly achieved harmonically or through angular melodic contours, or reiterated rhythmic ostinati. One of the simplest ways to increase tension on a particular chord is to place a piccolo a half step above a high violin note. The piccolo's power in this case is a wonder of acoustics. Each composer is unique in his use of these two monumental forces. Any attempt to categorically define all of the ways tension and motion are achieved would be impossible, but suffice to say that being aware of them as you listen to film scores can reveal a lot about the essence of the dramatic contour of a score.

OTHER ELEMENTS

In addition to motion and tension, there are other dramatic devices that you can listen for. Among these are:

1. the harmonic language (sweet, dissonant, quartal, tonal, twelve-tone).

2. if the amount of musical "data" expected for the audience to assimilate per second is appropriate, or could it be less and still accomplish the same effect (i.e., is the score too busy?)

3. the amount of neutral sound, where there is a conscious effort to minimize associations with clichés or musical connotations.

4. dialog clarity; does music get in the way?

5. whether the music enters or leaves to your taste. Would no music, or less music, suit you better?

6. whether the music confuses characterization or distracts the viewer (too many themes).

ANALYZE AN ENTIRE FILM SCORE

This can be a very laborious process if taken seriously, but there are important rewards for beginning film composers to analyze a film score in its entirety. With today's DVD format, it is simple to locate specific moments in a film. In your analysis, write down a short melodic fragment to identify each entrance of music, noting its start and end times, instrumentation, and the kind of variation treatment used (if any). Most importantly, note the dramatic use of the themes and their transformations. These observations can give you an overview of how many themes are used, how many times they occur, in what keys, and the overall time of the score vs. the entire film.

Most of the 60-odd films I have worked on generally have had about 25 to 30 cues, maybe four to five themes, with the overall duration of music from 40 to 60 minutes. Some films have very little music (ten to fifteen minutes) while others are nearly nonstop throughout. Regardless of the film, you should note if there is much variation of the themes; if so, to what dramatic purpose? What connections does the composer make in his reuse of themes? Is there sufficient rhythmic contrast for an interesting score, could it stand alone as music only? Was there too much music or not enough? These kinds of questions can reveal not only the diverse nature of one film score to the next, but also certain common grounds that film scores may share. This kind of project, because of its large scope, might best be done by several people.

Also, with DVDs you can sometimes find included among the extra features such things as interviews with composers about how a score was conceived (e.g., Hans Zimmer on the *Gladiator* DVD). Some, notably those by Danny Elfman, even allow you to play the movie with score only.

FILM SCORING STUDY PROGRAMS

Some colleges are beginning to encourage the study of film scoring in their academic confines, most notably USC, UCLA, New York University, and Berklee College of Music. The benefits of studying in this environment are many:

1. You get a feel for the current state of the art and what techniques are available to make your writing fast and effective.

2. You can compare your abilities to others with the same interest.

3. You have your work evaluated by professionals in the field, and often famous guests from the filmmaking world are invited to talk and work with the students.

4. You make contacts and friends for future work possibilities (networking).

You can find a complete bibliography of books to date on film music at the Film International Web site (**www.filmint.nu/eng.html**), compiled by Gillian Anderson and Ronald H. Sadoff, titled Music and Image Bibliography.

Business 12

For beginning film score composers, as with most creative artists, the start of your career is the time when you do anything and everything you can in order to start building a resume that will move you up the food chain. Never say no to any job, whether you like it or not, because any one job is not an end in itself but the beginning of what could be other contacts that lead to even more contacts, and so on. The particulars of the job itself are unimportant as long as there are redeeming values of some kind. You must do everything possible to put yourself in the position of meeting and hopefully working with those in the film business.

I have seen composers become so selective in the jobs they will accept that eventually no one calls them. Unless you are born with the proverbial silver spoon in your mouth, try greeting every gig with, "Sure I'd love to," and get through it to get to the next one that might be more to your liking. Even the biggest film composers have found themselves, on occasion, in situations where it became apparent that the director did not want an original score but simply wanted them to work with a previous composer's themes, to vary and shape them into final form. Some people might get so incensed by this they would stomp out in a rage of pride, saying, "It's my score or none." It's much better to be known as a talented person who can be called to cheerfully come to the rescue of almost any musical situation and be counted on to produce good work. This is a much more fruitful approach to building a career that I think will pay off in the long run.

And, never, ever, accept a gig, only to abandon it when a better one comes along. Word will eventually get around that you are not reliable. If you want to cover more than what you can individually handle, by all means take all the jobs you are offered and then subcontract some of it to trusted friends. That way everyone is happy and you have fulfilled your obligations.

You want all of your clients to feel you are there only for them. Don't mention how busy you are with other projects or say that you'll try to "squeeze them in." Let them think theirs is the only thing you are working on. Clients occasionally need reassurance, and it can be in the form of reciting to them a simple phrase. I knew one composer whose way of calming an anxious director was to say many times, "I know precisely what to do."

Another memorable line that can be used to placate clients I learned from a contractor, who would say, the minute a client became nervous that his work was not getting done, "I'm on your side," or, "Listen, I love my job." I don't know exactly what these things meant in context, but they seem to have gotten him through many a rough situation because I heard him use them a lot.

Of course, like everything else, there is a price to pay for saying yes to everyone and every job, and that is, not everything will go smoothly. There will be delays, screwups, people you trust who don't come through for you, etc., but whatever horror stories arise, never tell your client about the tough time you may be having. No one is interested in hearing how you had to stay up all night to get his work done, how your computer crashed and you sent it to California to be fixed, or how, in the middle of all this, your wife left you.

When things seem too much to bear, just go for a walk or pet the dog and come back with a fresh mind. Only the really "big players" have the luxury of complaining in public and having people listen. There are many talented musicians who can take your place in a flash, so don't give anyone the slightest reason not to hire you again.

WHAT TO CHARGE

When I am asked by a composer or orchestrator what they should charge for a project (not Hollywood films, of course, but smaller projects), it's difficult to answer, not knowing their relationship to the client, who is paying (an individual or a company), what the usage of their music will be, and so on. My advice is to first ask for the client's music budget. If the client says they don't have one, ask what they have paid in the past for comparable projects (hopefully this is not their first one). If that fee is acceptable, and you like the client and want to build a relationship, then do it, no matter how small the fee. Get in the door, and the next time see about making more money.

Sometimes no money but a great credit is worth it. Other times, a lot of money and no credit is worth it. And if it's a favor, you might get no money *and* no credit. But hopefully, with every project, you will be making contacts that might come back in bigger ways three years from now. If you could write your first professional-quality feature film score for no money except to cover expenses, you would be a fool not to do it, because then you would have that all-important first film to show agents and future clients. You would be getting "paid in spades," just no money.

CLIENTS

Clients come in many sizes, shapes, and varieties. Some you love and will do anything for. Others you respect and don't mind working with. And there are those you never want to see again. Because of these qualities, you might consider charging different amounts of money in each case. In most businesses, especially the creative arts, there is definitely not any *prix fixe* for anything. You charge differently according to:

1. who is paying? (your uncle Otis or Paramount)

2. how they will use your music? (one time or many, on TV or just at the local Elks Club)

3. will you get royalties or a percentage of the profits? (this could lower your initial fee)

Accordingly, you will then charge different clients different rates.

1. Some pay what they can (which can be zero), and if the benefits are more than monetary, that can work.

2. Some pay about half the best rate, because they are neither rich nor poor, and you probably want to work for them again, as opposed to the one mentioned above.

3. Some pay top dollar without royalties or residuals.

4. And last, and best of all, some pay top dollar and residuals.

All are good, in their own way.

PACKAGE DEALS

It is not uncommon for a composer to be expected to produce an entire film score for one lump sum that includes everything. It sounds like a lot of money at first—$100,000, $200,000, or more—but when you start adding up the possible costs, the composer's share can dwindle very quickly. You have to consider which of the following you want to pay for:

Musicians (union jobs require you to pay pension and health benefits)
Orchestrator
Contractor (including double or triple scale for some musicians)
Conductor
Copyist (supplies, messengers, assistants)
Payroll service
Cartage of instruments (harp, percussion)
Rental of recording studio, mixer, mixer assistants, equipment rental, etc.
Mixing time and transfer costs
Miscellaneous (piano tuning, overdub sessions, catering for musicians, etc.)

This all sounds very daunting to figure out. Because you will create a synth score first anyway, to cut down on costs you could:

1. use mainly a synth score with some live players for sweetening.

2. use a live orchestra (with some synth sweetening or none).

3. leave the score as a synth score.

Obviously, it is to your advantage to pass all expenses on to the film company when possible. If they say their music budget is not big enough to cover everything, ask if there are some categories other than music that specific expenses could be allocated to, since there are many different departments in a film's budget. For example, it might be possible for some of your travel or rental expenses to be taken from other parts of the budget.

Again, first time composers should not look for what to charge as much as what it is they will be getting from the experience, and that does not always have a monetary value.

CONTRACTS

Smaller projects may not require contracts, though if any sizable amount of money is to change hands (from theirs to yours), it might be best to have a contract drawn up by a lawyer, regardless of the stature of the project. A film composer agent might do this for you, which would be a good way to introduce yourself to him and show that you can be an asset and not a liability.

A contract describing your work for a film company should include some mention of the timeline for the project's beginning and end. You can expect that rewrites might be asked for days or even weeks beyond the stated date of completion, but even these have to have an end date; otherwise, you could be spending too much time trying to please a director who might be impossible to please. This occasionally happens when a director can't decide what score he wants or if there is disagreement between the director and producers about whose film they are making. Have your lawyer check any contracts with film studios before you sign them to make sure you are on solid ground.

There is a story about Philip Glass writing a score for the documentary filmmaker Errol Morris, where Mr. Glass completed what he thought was the final music cue and left town for his next job. A few days later, Mr. Morris was at his door saying, "There are a few more cues I want you to do." To prevent this, spell out in your contract a date beyond which you cannot go. If the film still needs work beyond that point, then a new contract will be negotiated for the additional work, your schedule permitting.

It is wise to include in your contract the kinds of expenses you will *not* be liable for, such as the costs for an orchestrator, mixer, and music editor, plus the kinds of expenses they will incur when they travel (car rental, hotel, per diem, etc.). This avoids any incidents such as a hotel telling the orchestrator he owes them $3,500 for his week's stay, when he thought the film company would be covering it.

The film company also requests contracts. Usually the company asks the composer (occasionally the orchestrator) to sign an indemnification agreement promising that the music created is original and any lawsuits from third parties to the contrary will be litigated at the composer's expense. This is usually a formality, as I've never heard of any suits over film scores (pop tunes, yes). So don't be alarmed at this, unless, of course, you are asked to mimic a previously existing score by a big-name composer (whom they wanted instead of you, but couldn't afford). Then you should proceed very carefully and possibly mimic textures but not actual themes, going for a general feel but not literal rip-off .

When asked to do this kind of "sound-alike" score, you might check about whether the previous film score's themes were original or whether the composer took some or all of them from a public domain source (as with the *Rocky* theme, the beginning part of which was a very old classical trumpet piece).

THE MUSICIAN'S UNION

Most all Hollywood films use union members throughout their crew and, as an orchestrator, I am a member of the musician's union and pay work dues for each check I receive through them. Some of the benefits of belonging to the union include the Special Payments Fund, which pays royalties to musicians listed on the film contracts for reuse made of the film (TV, CD, DVD, etc.). Also, when questions arise as to what or how to charge for certain services, your local union can usually advise you how to proceed. Different rate schedules apply for each kind of service, and they change frequently, so before quoting figures you should contact the union for the most current ones. The union has established minimum scale amounts for each service; however, it is common that these minimums are exceeded. Also, the union provides health benefits and a pension plan funded by a percentage of your scale wages on each contract paid by your various employers.

CREDITS

And so, we finally come to that item which we all, at least initially, crave the most: credit, or acknowledgment, for what we do. It is best if we get it in the form of big letters on the screen, even if it does come after the third assistant caterer. If I have a contract as orchestrator, my credit size and place in the scroll is never stated. With the best people I work for, sometimes it just shows up; they are professional and courteous about such things. And if it is not there, that's okay too.

The best credit of all is simply to know I have been a part of many thrilling film projects, working with amazingly talented people. I feel, in the writer Garrison Keillor's phrase, "happy to be here." It's a very good place to be. "I love my job," "I'm on your side," and "I know precisely what to do."

Final notes

The resources available to film composers today are better than ever. Sophisticated computer software gives them the ability to create very credible synth mockups for auditioning their work, and the explosion of filmmaking in general means more possibilities for practicing their craft. All the tools we could want are easily available and common to us all. It is how we use them that is the unknown quantity in the equation.

I want to summarize what I believe are the most important things to keep in mind as you begin working.

ASK QUESTIONS IN ADVANCE

In all of your dealings with directors, film companies, recording studios, musicians, etc., be sure you understand what their expectations are, whether it concerns a musician's part, your bill, the mixer's experience, or how much time you are to spend on a project. With everyone you encounter, be sure you know in advance what their expectations are, so there are no misunderstandings later. Once a job is complete, the tone of communication can be very different; no one wants to talk about old news, so settle important matters before the fact and it will save you many problems later on. Especially with bills, keep in touch with those paying you every two weeks or so to keep your file somewhere near the top of their pile of invoices.

ASSUME NOTHING

It is good business practice to take nothing for granted. Don't be a chronic annoyance to anyone, but simply reassure yourself that all details are covered and nothing is left to chance. You will need all the time you have for doing your job. Having to fix misunderstandings after the fact only takes away from more important things. From how many hours you have to record to having the piano tuned, leave nothing to chance.

Do Not Cut Corners

Whether in the amount of work it takes to compose twelve rewrites, the number of phone calls necessary to maintain a good working relationship with your colleagues, or the amount of paper required to print your parts, if you begin adopting a philosophy of cutting corners, it will hurt you. It is a slippery slope that never ends. So always say to yourself, when confronted with more than you expected, that you will do the most professional job you know how, whatever it takes. A young assistant engineer taught me this one morning at 8 a.m. as I was entering a studio and he was leaving. When I asked if he had been there all night, he just smiled and said, "Whatever it takes."

Be Concise and Focused

In your work and business relationships, it is wise to develop an attitude of economy and focus. Do your toughest work when you can best concentrate so time is not wasted. When you speak with your colleagues, be concise and to the point. When I'm tired, I do those things that require the least amount of brain-power, such as layouts, timings, printing sketches, etc., saving the thoughtful work for when I am fresh. When I call someone about business, I respectfully wait until the call is necessary before dialing, to avoid situations like, "Let me see, why did I call you?" This kind of work ethic will not only benefit you but will be appreciated by those you deal with.

Have Opinions

If you tend to be shy, Hollywood is not the place to exhibit it. In all of your dealings, you should present your opinions in an open but respectful way. If you feel you are asked to do something that strikes you as pointless and misguided, state your position calmly and succinctly. Perhaps you can do what you are asked, but also do another version of what you think would be best, and let your position be known. Very often directors are unsure of what they want and welcome input from the composer. So don't hesitate to speak up.

Take Your Time

There will be many times when you will be prodded to do something quickly. Film studios or directors want to hear themes tomorrow, you have five minutes to fix and record the last cue before the band leaves, you get a new edit of the film the night before you begin recording—all of these things can and will happen. An attitude of calm, focused expediency is something we could all do well to adopt. Work as fast as you can without losing control of the decision-making process that will ensure your best work. It is not necessary to yell at those requesting the impossible, but assure them that you are working as diligently as possible. That's all anyone can do. If you can, call someone to help you out, by all means. The first priority is to get the job done, and frequently the film company will cover the expense. Just make sure you ask up-front.

BE CALM AND COURTEOUS

While you are trying to work, you will encounter many distractions. Amid a barrage of phone calls from a studio secretary who is booking your flight reservations, a director who wants a rewrite of the last three cues, a producer who hasn't liked anything he's heard so far, you should try your best to deal with these things in as calm a manner as possible. It is easier on the phone, because after you hang up you can scream all the obscenities you want at the wall to relieve your anger. They are simply doing their jobs. It is just unfortunate for you that, at the moment, all of their jobs involve calling you. Just relax, and think of how grateful they will be when they hear your score.

BE PREPARED FOR REJECTION

Rest assured, anyone who has ever written a film score has experienced rejection. From film scores being thrown out in their entirety, to replacement of certain cues by temp tracks or other composers, to requests by the studio or directors for more and more rewrites, you will certainly have to deal with those times when your music simply is not what the listener had in mind. Obviously, it is most difficult to accept when you disagree with the musical judgment of the person offering the criticism. Part of your job is to take it in stride and simply remedy the situation with something they will approve. While this may be the most unpleasant thing about film scoring, it is also the most common, so do not be surprised when it happens and take comfort in the fact that you are not alone.

KEEP MOVING

Whether you are composing, trying to get legit players to swing, or trying to resolve procedural issues with a director, you must find ways of maintaining progress in your work. Give each matter the time it deserves, and move on. There is no time for writer's block or arguing about some irresolvable matter. If necessary, do alternate versions of cues to please opposing factions, or leave out problematic parts while recording and overdub later. In other words, do not dwell too much on any one thing or you will get yourself in a terrible bind. The entire structure and budget of a film revolve around the score being completed within a certain time frame, and this is usually a very hard and fast deadline. No one will be interested in hearing why you may need extra time or money. It is important to make every effort to pace yourself and stay on schedule.

IT'S ALL GOOD

Surprisingly, I've had students who have very strong likes and dislikes about the kind of films they want to score. This is fine as long as someone else is paying the bills for you, since what you choose to work on doesn't affect your income. But in the real world, if you need to make a living, you will not be helping your career by turning down work because you don't like a certain kind of film. The saying, "It's all good," means to maintain an active career where your name is in circulation and you have a reputation for doing good work, taking all the work you can and doing your very best no matter what the job. Successful film composers usually have a wide range of abilities and can turn their style on almost any kind of film genre and come up with a successful score. I have seen talented musicians reject so much work that eventually no one calls. So, at least until you have a secure reputation and can be selective, try accepting all the challenges you can and make the most of them. You might discover abilities in areas you never thought you had.

Hopefully, with some luck and the kindness of strangers, you will be on your way to enjoying all the best that the film world has to offer.

Resources

*T*here's always more to learn about film scoring. Consult the following resources for more information.

FILM / MUSIC SCHOOLS

To learn more about music composition and the business of film production, there are a multitude of educational facilities around the world that are ready to train you. To learn the craft of composition, consider a college with a school of music. At some facilities, film scoring classes are actually available through their film studies program. Research the following options to see which is right for you.

The Art Institute of Vancouver - Burnaby
3264 Beta Ave.
Burnaby, BC V5G 4K4
Canada
Tel: 604-298-5400
aivan.artinstitutes.edu
Notes: Offers a Music For Television & Film course through the Recording Arts program.

American University

School of Visual Media
440 Massachusetts Ave. NW
Washington, D.C. 20016
Tel: 202-885-2060
www.american.edu

Notes: The School of Visual Media offers a variety of relevant classes, as well as the opportunity to spend a semester in Prague studying at the Academy of Dramatic Arts in Prague (FAMU).

ASCAP Film Scoring Workshop

7920 W. Sunset Boulevard, Third Floor
Los Angeles, CA 90046
Tel: 323-883-1000
www.ascap.com/calendar

Notes: ASCAP offers a series of lectures offering real-world advice from industry executives, agents, attorneys, composers, and studio musicians. Participants also have the opportunity to record an original composition on a major studio scoring stage with a group of "A list" Hollywood professionals, including a 40-piece orchestra, a legendary scoring mixer, and professional composers and music editors acting as coaches and mentors.

Berklee College of Music

1140 Boylston Street
Boston, MA 02215
Tel: 617-266-1400
www.berklee.edu

Notes: Berklee offers a host of composition and film scoring courses.

BMI

320 West 57th Street
New York, NY 10019-3790
Tle: 212-586-2000
www.bmi.com

Notes: BMI offers workshops for those interesting in scoring for films.

Boston University

College of Communication

640 Commonwealth Avenue

Boston, MA 02215

Tel: 617-353-3450

www.bu.edu

Notes: Take BU's Sound Design for Film and Television course through the College of Communications.

California State University at Long Beach

College of the Arts

1250 Bellflower Blvd.

Long Beach, CA 90804

Tel: 562-985-4364

www.csulb.edu

Notes: Check out the offerings from the Film & Electronic Arts program in the College of the Arts.

Chapman University

School of Film & Television

School of Music

One University Dr.

Cecil B. DeMille Hall

Orange, CA 92866

Tel: 714-997-6765

www.chapman.edu

Notes: You'll find relevant coursework in both the School of Film & Television and the School of Music.

Columbia College Chicago

Semester in LA

600 South Michigan Avenue

Chicago, IL 60605

Tel: 312-663-1600

www.filmatcolumbia.com

Notes: Columbia's Semester in LA, a five-week, immersion program and covers producing, directing, screenwriting, costuming, styling and wardrobe management, adaption-screenwriting, TV pilot development, writing the TV sitcom, entertainment public relations and marketing, and music composition.

Columbia University

Film-School of the Arts
305 Dodge
Mailcode 1808
2960 Broadway
New York, NY 10027
Tel: 212-854-2875
www.columbia.edu

Notes: Columbia University's program combines directing, writing, and producing with technical training and history/theory to provide students with a deep understanding of the principles and practice of dramatic narrative.

Film Music Institute

11601 Wilshire Boulevard
Suite 500
Los Angeles, CA 90025
Tel: 310-575-1820
www.filmmusicinstitute.com

Notes: Offers professional level courses for the film, television, and multimedia music industry taught by working industry pros who focus on specific tools, techniques, strategies, and skills. Classes are held in various locations in Los Angeles and New York.

Florida State University

The Film School
University Center 3100A
Tallahassee, FL 32306
Tel: 850-644-7728
www.filmschool.fsu.edu

Notes: Operates its main studios in Tallahassee and its music recording stage and back-lot property in Quincy, Florida.

Full Sail Real World Education

3300 University Blvd.
Winter Park, FL 32792
Tel: 800-226-7625
www.fullsail.com

Notes: Its Film program offers an Associate of Science degree.

Hofstra University

Music Department
Emily Lowe Hall, 112 Hofstra U.
Hempstead, NY 11549
Tel: 516-463-4931
www.hofstra.edu/academics/hclas/

Notes: Relevant courses offered in the Composition and Commercial Music departments.

Institute of Audio Research

64 University Place
New York, NY 10003
Tel: 212-777-8550
www.audioschool.com

Notes: Offers technical audio courses for post-production and recording studio-based careers.

Johns Hopkins University

Film & Media Studies
3400 N. Charles St., Gilman 453
Baltimore, MD 21218
Tel: 410-516-5048
www.jhu.edu/~film_media

Notes: Film and Media Studies is an interdisciplinary program incorporating courses in film history and theory, film and digital video production, and screen-writing.

Loyola Marymount University

School of Film + TV
1 LMU Drive
Los Angeles, CA 90045
Tel: 310-338-2700
www.lmu.edu

Notes: Offers undergraduate and graduate studies in Animation, Film Production, Recording Arts, Screenwriting, and Film and Video Production.

MusicTech College

Music for Motion Imaging
19 Exchange Street East
Saint Paul, MN 55101
Tel: 800-594-9500
www.musictech.edu

Notes: Offers many degrees, including Motion Imaging which includes an aggressive music composition tract.

New York University

Music & Performing Arts Professions
35 West 4th St., Room 777
New York, NY 10012
Tel: 212-998-5424
www.nyu.edu/education/music/mfilm/

Notes: Scoring for Film and Multimedia is a 45-point masters level curriculum designed within programs for Music Composition and Music Technology. The Music Composition program places an emphasis on composing for film, TV, and multimedia, including interactive performance, silent film, multimedia, web-based media.

Pacific Northwest Film Scoring Program

8403 SE 53rd Place
Mercer Island, WA 98040
Tel: 800-546-8611
www.pnwfilmmusic.com

Notes: A renown program run by two time Emmy Award-winning composer/arranger/conductor Hummie Mann that provides training to music composition students, composers and others interested in the art of modern film scoring.

SAE Institute of Technology

1293 Broadway, 9th floor
New York, NY 10001
Tel: 212-944-9121
www.sae.edu

Notes: Offers training programs in audio, multimedia, and digital film.

Selkirk College
Film Scoring Department
301 Frank Beinder Way
Castlegar, B.C. V1N 3J1
Canada
Tel: 250-505-1362
www.selkirk.bc.ca

Notes: An entire film scoring department offers degree programs at this Canadian college.

Trebas Institute
Toronto Campus
149 College Street
Toronto, ON M5T 1P5
Canada
Tel: (416) 966-3066
www.trebas.com

Notes: Trebas offers many technical courses that relate to the film, TV, and video production industries.

Trebas Institute
550 Sherbrooke Street W.,
6th Floor, East Tower,
Montreal, Quebec H3A 1B9
Canada
Tel: (514) 845-4141
www.trebas.com

UCLA Extension Entertainment Studies
10995 Le Conte Ave., Room 437
Los Angeles, CA 90024
Tel: (310) 825-9064
www. uclaextension.org/entertainmentstudies

Notes: A well-respected program for film scoring and composition.

University of Alabama
School of Music
Box 870366
Tuscaloosa, AL 35487
Tel: 205-348-1476
www.bama.ua.edu/~twolfe/film1.htm

Notes: A solid music program with many courses that will help aspiring film composers achieve their career goals.

University of California at San Diego
Center for Research in Computing & the Arts
9500 Gilman Drive, Room 408
La Jolla, CA 92093
Tel: 858-534-4383
www.ucsd.edu

Notes: Several courses that are pertinent to those seeking knowledge in the music for film/TV arena.

University of North Alabama
Entertainment Industry Center / Music Dept.
UNA Box 5040
Florence, AL 35632
Tel: 256-765-4361
www2.una.edu/entertainment

Notes: A contemporary music program offering courses in music publishing, songwriting, production, and more.

University of Texas at Austin
Department of Radio, TV, and Film
CMA 6.118
Austin, TX 78712
Tel: 512-471-4071
www.utexas.edu/coc/rtf

Notes: A broad-based education in the radio, TV, and film industries.

USC Thornton School of Music
University Park - UUC 218
Los Angeles, CA 90089
Tel: 800-872-2213
www.usc.edu/music
Notes: The School of Music offers a variety of courses that are pertinent to composers wishing to build a film career.

PROFESSIONAL SOCIETIES AND ORGANIZATIONS

American Composers Forum of Los Angeles
www.composers.la

American Federation of Musicians
www.afm.org

American Federation of Television & Radio Artists (AFTRA)
www.aftra.com

American Film Institute
www.afi.com

American Music Conference
www.amc-music.org

Academy of Motion Picture Arts & Sciences (AMPAS)
www.oscars.org/index.html

Academy of Television Arts & Sciences
www.emmys.com

ASCAP
www.ascap.com

BMI
www.bmi.com

British Academy of Film and Television Arts
www.bafta.org

Directors Guild of America
www.dga.org

Film Music Society
www.filmmusicsociety.org

Film Score Rundowns
www.comcen.com.au/~agfam/rundowns/index.html

Game Audio Network Guild
www.audiogang.org

The Henry Mancini Institute
www.manciniinstitute.org

IATSE
www.iatse.com

Independent Feature Project
www.ifp.org

Meet the Composer
www.meetthecomposer.org

Motion Picture Editors Guild
IATSE Local 700
www.editorsguild.com

MPSE
Motion Picture Sound Editors
www.mpse.org

The Mr. Holland's Opus Foundation
www.mhopus.org

National Academy of Recording Arts & Sciences (NARAS)
www.grammy.com

Professional Musicians Local 47, AFM
www.promusic47.org

Recording Musicians Association LA
www.rmala.org

Screen Actors Guild (SAG)
www.sag.org

SESAC

www.sesac.com

The Society of Composers & Lyricists

www.thescl.com/site/scl/

Songwriters Guild of America

www.songwritersguild.com

Writers Guild of America (WGA)

www.wga.org

Women in Film

www.wif.org

SUGGESTED SCORES TO STUDY

The following list includes just a few outstanding film scores. It is interesting that what are considered "great films" are not always the ones we necessarily love the most—and vice versa. I remember Victor Young's score for Around the World in Eighty Days as absolutely stunning, but the film itself is not exactly great drama. This list has mostly "universal favorites" and a few personal ones of mine:

Film	Composer	Year
Amarcord	Nina Rota	1973
Ben Hur	Miklos Rozsa	1959
Casablanca	Max Steiner	1942
Chinatown	Jerry Goldsmith	1974
Cinema Paradiso	Ennio Morricone	1989
The Deer Hunter	Stanley Myers	1978
Doctor Zhivago	Maurice Jarre	1965
Dressed To Kill	Pino Donaggio	1980
El Cid	Miklos Rozsa	1961
Far From Heaven	Elmer Bernstein	2002
The Godfather	Nina Rota	1972
Goldfinger	John Barry	1964
The Good Bad & The Ugly	Ennio Morricone	1966
The Heiress	Aaron Copland	1949
High Noon	Dmitri Tiomkin	1952
La dolce vita	Nina Rota	1960
Lawrence of Arabia	Maurice Jarre	1962
The Magnificent Ambersons	Bernard Herrmann	1942
The Magnificent Seven	Elmer Bernstein	1960
The Man Who Would Be King	Maurice Jarre	1975
The Natural	Randy Newman	1984
North By Northwest	Bernard Herrmann	1959
The Old Man and the Sea	Dmitri Tiomkin	1958
On The Waterfront	Leonard Bernstein	1954
Our Town	Aaron Copland	1940
The Pawnbroker	Quincy Jones	1964
Planet of the Apes	Jerry Goldsmith	1968
Psycho	Bernard Herrmann	1960
Silence of the Lambs	Howard Shore	1991
Silverado	Bruce Broughton	1985

Spider	Howard Shore	2002
Star Wars	John Williams	1977
Streetcar Named Desire	Alex North	1951
Touch of Evil	Henry Mancini	1958
The Untouchables	Ennio Morricone	1987
Vertigo	Bernard Herrmann	1958

SUGGESTED READING

Adler, Samuel. *Study of Orchestration,* New York: W.W. Norton & Company, 2002.

Bell, David A. *Getting the Best Score for Your Film: A Filmmakers' Guide to Music Scoring,* Los Angeles: Silman-James Press, 1994.

Black, Dave and Gerou, Tom. *Essential Dictionary of Orchestration,* Van Nuys, CA: Alfred Publishing Company, 1998.

Burt, George. *The Art of Film Music,* Boston: Northeastern University Press, 1996.

Cooper, David. *Bernard Herrmann's Vertico: A Film Score Handbook,* Westport, CT: Greenwood Press, 2001.

Davis, Richard. *Complete Guide to Film Scoring: The Art and Business of Writing Music for Movies and TV,* Boston: Berklee Press, 2000.

Fisher, Jeff. *How to Make Money Scoring Soundtracks and Jingles,* Emeryville, CA: MixBooks, 1997.

Forsyth, Cecil. *Orchestration,* Mineola, NY: Dover Publications, 1982.

Hagen, Earle. *Advanced Techniques for Film Scoring,* Van Nuys, CA: Alfred Publishing Company, 1990.

Karlin, Fred and Wright, Doris. *On the Track: A Guide to Contemporary Film Scoring,* New York: Routledge, 2003.

Morgan, David. *Knowing the Score: Film Composers Talk About the Art, Craft, Blood, Sweat, and Tears of Writing Music for Cinema,* New York: HarperEntertainment, 2000.

Northam, Mark and Miller, Lisa Anne. *Film and Television Composer's Resource Guide: The Complete Guide to Organizing and Building Your Business,* New York: Hal Leonard, 1998.

Prendergast, Roy M. *Film Music: A Neglected Art: A Critical Study of Music in Films,* New York: W.W. Norton & Company, 1992.

Ray, Don B. *The Orchestration Handbook: The Essential Guide to Every Instrument in the Orchestra,* New York: Hal Leonard, 2000.

Rimsky-Korsakov. *Principles for Orchestration,* Mineola, NY: Dover Publications, 1964.

Rona, Jeff. *The Reel World: Scoring for Pictures,* San Francisco: Backbeat Books, 2001.

Schelle, Michael. *The Score: Interviews With Film Composers,* Los Angeles: Silman-James Press, 1999.

In addition, a complete bibliography of books on film music exists at the Web site Film International (www.filmint.nu/eng/html) entitled *Music and Image Bibliography.*

WEB SITES

Film International
www.filmint.nu/eng.html
Music and image bibliography—complete list of books and film music

Internet Archives' Movie Archives
www.archive.org/movies/movies.php
Free films to download

SoundtrackNet
www.soundtrack.net/representation
A good list of film composers' agents

Film Music Network
www.filmmusic.net and www.filmmusicjobs.com
Good links and industry directories, composing job sources (for a fee)

Film Music Magazine
www.filmmusicmag.com
Online version of the magazine by Film Music Network

The Film Music Society
www.filmmusicsociety.org
Great links and articles

Film Score Monthly
www.filmscoremonthly.com
Online magazine with articles and CD, video, and book reviews

FilmSound.org
www.filmsound.org/filmmusic
Focuses mainly on sound design, but also a good bibliography and articles

Filmtracks
www.filmtracks.com
Soundtrack reviews

Field of Dreams — Online Film Music Publication
www.fod-online.com
Mostly composer interviews

Hollywood Reporter
www.hollywoodreporter.com
General movie and TV news; lists films in progress (for a fee)

The Internet Movie Database
www.imdb.com
The best site for cast and crew information; also films in progress list for a fee (IMDBpro), good glossary of cinematic terms, and links to film schools

Movie Music
www.moviemusic.com
Film soundtrack directory, good links to magazines, concerts, and composer sites

MovieWave
www.moviewave.net
Soundtrack reviews

Music From the Movies
www.musicfromthemovies.com
Film music news, reviews, and articles

TrackSounds
www.tracksounds.com
Soundtrack reviews, news, and composer interviews.

Note: For additional resources, check the "links" section of the above Web sites.

Glossary

accelerando   Becoming faster.

accidental   A sharp or flat occurring in printed music that is not in the designated key signature.

alberti   A type of accompaniment, usually in eighth-notes, which outlines a chord (e.g., Mozart's piano sonata K.545).

analog   To a musician in a recording studio, this refers to an older method of sound recording using audio tape, as opposed to digital sound stored in a computer.

arpeggi   Playing notes of a chord (usually from bottom to top) in rapid succession.

arranging   Writing a musical score from a melody or sketch with discretion taken in regard to harmony, tempo, length, instrumentation, and general character. See comparison with "orchestration."

articulation   Markings placed above or below written musical notes to indicate the attack and release characteristics of the note, various gradations of short, long, or slurred.

atonal   A non-triadic harmonic basis for music that does not employ the traditional principles of chord structure or movement and very often appears to have no "tonal" center or "home base."

AV   An abbreviation for "audio-visual."

baffle   A temporary acoustical wall or screen positioned in a recording studio to block sound to or from a certain area.

bar (measure)   A division of music into groups of usually two, three, or four beats with the strongest beat being the first of each group.

baton   A stick of some eight to 20 inches in length used by a conductor when leading a musical ensemble to make his beat movements more easily seen.

bleeding   In a recording situation, the sound of an instrument traveling to mics other than its own.

booth   The control room of a recording studio.

bowing   With string instruments, slurs indicating those notes which are to be played together smoothly in one bow stroke.

CD   Compact disc. A digitally encoded disc capable of containing more than one hour of music at a sampling frequency of 44.1 kHz.

chord symbol   Letter/number abbreviations for musical chords—e.g., Cm7(♭5) used mostly by pop/jazz musicians.

click   A repeated non-pitched sound used as a guide to the tempo of a musical score, produced by a sequencer program (previously by a metronome or click track box)

composer   Person who writes or performs original music.

concert score   "C" score, a musical score showing all instruments' parts at the pitches where they actually sound.

conductor   The musical leader of a musical ensemble who guides the musicians by means of arm movements.

contractor   The person who hires the musicians for a musical performance.

contrapuntal   Two or more distinct melodies played at once, prominent in Baroque music, fugues in particular.

controller   Any electronic musical instrument that can be plugged into a sound module to trigger electronic sounds. Every electronic keyboard made today has a MIDI output jack enabling it to be a controller for playing electronic sounds.

copyist (music)   The person who creates separate parts from the composer/orchestrator's score for each musician of an orchestra.

crescendo   Becoming louder.

cue   Music accompanying a film scene, denoted by the reel number, letter M, and cue number. Thus, 3M7 means reel 3, music cue 7.

cue system   The headset monitoring system and talkback mics in a recording studio that allow musicians, conductor, and those in the control room to communicate with each other.

demo   A musical sound recording used for demonstration purposes.

diminuendo   Becoming softer.

director   The person responsible for coordinating all aspects of a film—actors, crew, music etc.

divisi   A term instructing string players to divide the notes on their musical stave into separate parts.

doubling   The playing of the same musical notes by more than one instrument.

downbeat   The very first strong beat of a musical score.

dub   To make a copy of any video or music source. Also, the copy itself.

DVD   Digital versatile disc, the primary commercial method of storing and playing back film, replacing videotape. Holds nearly five gigabytes of information.

dynamics   Letter indications of the degree of loudness and softness in a musical score.

film scoring   The process of creating music to accompany a film.

Finale A professional music notation program. Also, Sibelius.

glissandi The smooth gliding from note to note, as in a harp playing a "sweep" from low to high notes.

harmonic rhythm The rhythm at which musical chords change.

harmonics One of a series of faint tones created above the fundamental tone of a musical instrument.

hits In film scoring parlance, where the music and image coincide for emphasis.

intonation The pitch of a musical instrument. "The intonation is off" means instruments are playing out of tune.

key signature The sharps or flats indicated at the beginning of a line of a musical score indicating the key of the music.

leakage In a recording studio, the undesirable sound coming from the musicians' headsets into the mics.

ledger lines Lines above or below a staff of music to indicate notes which fall outside the range of the staff itself.

legato An indication to a musician to play notes in a smooth and connected way without break.

legit An abbreviation for "legitimate" referring usually to a musician whose experience and training has been only the music of the classical Western European tradition.

leitmotif A musical motive or theme used to characterize a particular character, idea, place or situation in a dramatic score.

lift A part of a musical score that has been copied from another part of the same score, very common in film music where the music for one scene is used for that of another.

locked film A film in which the editing is complete and the sequence of scenes and their contents will remain as is.

lock to picture When synchronizing music to a video tape, the point at which the tape and music tracks become "in sync."

markers Short comments placed above music sequencer tracks "marking" important musical/visual moments.

meter signature The numbers at the beginning of a musical staff indicating how the beats are grouped, usually $\frac{2}{4}$, $\frac{3}{4}$, $\frac{4}{4}$, etc.

metronome marking (M.M.) Numbers placed at the beginning of a musical score to indicate the musical tempo by noting how many beats occur per minute for a certain note value (e.g., quarter note = 100 means there will be a tempo of 100 such beats per minute).

mic Abbreviation for microphone.

MIDI Musical Instrument Digital Interface. In common usage, an interface that allows a musical instrument (called a controller) to communicate with a computer sequencer program. There are many lengthy descriptions of MIDI online of what it is and how it is used.

MIDI file
A computer file containing data created by a musical instrument controller (i.e., electronic keyboard).

MIDI sequence
A computer file within a sequencer program (i.e., Digital Performer or Logic) containing one or more tracks of music created by a MIDI controller to which are assigned variable electronic sounds. These sequences can be "locked" to picture so the music is always in perfect sync with a film.

mix
To adjust the relative volume balances between various tracks of recorded music. Also, in film production, to adjust the various levels of music, sound effects, and dialog in the "final mix" of a film.

mixer
The person responsible for everything coming into or out of a mixing console at a recording session.

mixing console
The board containing controls for all incoming sound from the microphones in a recording session.

mixing session
Where all music tracks are played, balanced, and saved for later inclusion in the final film mix.

mockup
An electronic emulation of a live orchestra by a synthesizer in a sequencer program such as Digital Performer.

modulation
To change key in the middle of a musical piece.

molto
Italian word used as an adjective in musical scores to mean "very." "Molto ritard" means a drastic slowing down.

MP3
A format that allows you to compress and store music files on your computer.

music editor
The person responsible for everything involving the synchronization of a musical score with a film.

orchestration
The interpretation of a musical sketch for a live orchestra, written on score paper showing all the instruments. The "orchestrator" is the person who takes a composer's sketch or MIDI file and writes a score playable by musicians.

ostinato
A repeated musical pattern that continues for a substantial number of measures.

overdub
Adding an instrument to a pre-existing musical track, as when percussion instruments add their parts to a musical score already recorded by an orchestra.

parts
Individual music prepared for each musician by the music copyist.

patch
A particular sound produced by a synthesizer, usually emulating a live instrument, i.e., a "flute" patch.

PDF file
A file in Portable Document Format, usually created in the computer program Adobe Acrobat. This universal format allows any document saved in it to be opened for viewing by nearly any computer in the world. Adobe Acrobat Reader is available free online.

period film   A film taking place in an identifiable historical period, i.e., Elizabethan, Medieval, etc.

phasing   A type of sound wave interaction. Congruent waves are said to be "in phase," The playing of identical synth patches will sometimes cancel each other to the extent that the overall sound is weaker than one patch alone

phrasing   The smoothly connected grouping of musical lines by slurs.

pizzicato   A string instrument device of plucking the strings with a finger as opposed to bowing.

playback   Listening to a recorded performance of music.

ponticello   Playing near the bridge of a string instrument. It gives an intense, sharp-edged sound common in horror films.

portamento   Smoothly sliding from one note to another.

pre-record   Tracks that are recorded before the current recording session.

presets   On synthesizer keyboards, electronic sounds predetermined and installed at the factory and easily accessed.

Punch-in (-out)   To begin recording within a pre-recorded track of music, deciding beforehand the exact places to enter and exit. In recording situations, this allows a mistake to be corrected by re-recording only a section of music, thereby leaving what could very well be an excellent performance other than the one place that is replaced.

pyramid   Most often with brass instruments, where the first low note is held while the next higher note is played and held, continuing with higher instruments until a full chord is sounding.

QuickTime   A current standard for the playback of video in a computer. QuickTime is easily downloaded for free onto any computer and will play video files saved to this format (Apple iMovie will save to this format).

quantize   The ability of a computer sequencer program to adjust rhythms to perfect synchronization.

reverb   Abbreviation for reverberation, the electronic or acoustical reinforcement of sound through the repletion of the sound in varying diminished degrees, in the manner of an echo. The degree of electronic reverb can be controlled, whereby natural reverb is the result of the space in which sound is produced, such as a cathedral or concert hall.

ritard   Short for ritardando. Becoming slower.

rough cut   A preliminary trial stage in the process of editing a film. Shots are laid out in approximate relationship to an end product but not yet finalized.

sampled sounds   The sounds of a live musical instrument created by recording (sampling) many different registers of that live instrument and using these actual recorded sounds to produce an emulation of that instrument. Sounds created in this way are superior to "patches" or electronically produced emulations of live instruments.

score To score means to write music to a film. A score can mean simply the musical sound for a film (soundtrack), or the written pages showing all the music for the instruments playing on horizontal musical staves.

segue To continue without pause to the next section.

sequencer A computer program capable of recording impulses from a MIDI controller (e.g., electronic keyboard) and storing them in various tracks to which can be assigned various synthesized sounds in the creation of a musical score. Sequences created in this manner can be "locked" to film so that they are always in sync with the picture.

session Recording music in a studio.

sforzando Suddenly loud. (*sfz*)

Sibelius A professional music notation program offered first in the U.S. in 1998 after being developed in the U.K.. It has a reputation for being far easier to use than its older rival, Finale.

slate The recorded identification of a particular performance of a film music cue by reel and take number.

slur Two or more musical notes played without break (legato).

SMPTE Society of Motion Picture and Television Engineers. Originally, a high-frequency signal that allowed the accurate "locking" of film audio and video equipment. Locator information was displayed as numbers (05:02:45:23 would mean 5 hours, two minutes, 45 seconds and 23 frames). More recently, when working with digital audio, just the visual part of the code is used, since the film and audio are stored in the same computer and do not need "locking."

sound module   An electronic box containing emulated musical sounds and used as the sound source in sequencer programs.

spiccato   An Italian term meaning "springing," or lightly bouncing from one note to another.

spot   To identify the specific scenes or points where music cues will take place.

spotting notes   A list of each scene's character, mood, music desired, and start and end points, primarily for use by the composer.

streamers   A vertical line moving across the video screen (left to right) superimposed on a video to show a conductor when a particular event is about to happen. The event location occurs when the streamer hits the right side of the screen.

suits   The executives of a film studio.

sul tasto   For string instruments, playing with the bow over the fingerboard.

sweeten   To add music to a pre-existing music track.

syncopation   The shifting of musical accents to the weak parts of beats, e.g., accenting the second eighth of a beat.

sync points   Those points of a film which are to be emphasized by a musical action.

synth   Abbreviation for "synthesizer," electronic sounds stored in a computer and triggered or played by an electronic controller, such as an electronic keyboard. "Synthesized" refers to musical sounds created in this manner.

tacet   To be silent, not play.

take   A single recorded performance of a musical piece.

tempo   Rate of speed of music, indicated by the M.M. (metronome marking).

temp track   Musical tracks temporarily placed into a film's soundtrack prior to the final original score.

tenuto   Musical notes that are played in a sustained fashion and held for their full rhythmic value.

transpose   To move music to a different key.

transposed score   A score that has all instruments written as they are for the individual players, not necessarily where the pitches actually sound.

tremolo   The rapid alternation of two musical notes.

tutti   An Italian word meaning "all," where all instruments are to play.

unison   Where instruments are to play the same notes.

VHS   Video home system, the conventional video tape format currently being replaced by DVD.

vibrato   A wavering effect of tone.

wild   Sounds recorded without reference to a video. Sounds that can later be "dropped in" to a film score at will.

wrong side of the bridge   On string instruments, playing with the bow on the other side of the bridge from where usually played. This produces a very harsh effect akin to "nails on a blackboard" and is enormously ominous when played by an entire string section.

In addition, there is a very good glossary of cinematic terms at the Web site **www.imdb.com** (Internet Movie Database).

OTHER TITLES FROM SCHIRMER TRADE BOOKS

MUSIC BUSINESS

Music Business Made Simple: A Guide to Becoming a Recording Artist by J.S. Rudsenske (softcover, 6 x 9, 144 pages, $14.95)

Music, Money, and Success: The Insider's Guide to Making Money in the Music Industry, 4th edition by Jeffrey Brabec and Todd Brabec (softcover, 6 x 9.25, 488 pages, $24.95)

The Fought the Law: Rock Music Goes to Court by Stan Soocher (hardcover, 6 x 9, 253 pages, $25.00)

RECORDING & PRODUCTION

Keep Your Gear Running: Electronics for Musicians by Patrick L. McKeen (softcover, 7 x 10, 264 pages with 111 b/w illustrations, $19.95)

Assistant Engineer Handbook: Gigs in the Recording Studio and Beyond by Sarah Jones (softcover, 7 x 10, 224 pages, $19.95)

The Sonar Insider by Craig Anderton (softcover, 7 x 10, 224 pages, $19.95)

Sonar 3: Mixing and Mastering by Craig Anderton (softcover, 7 x 10, 460 pages, $50.00)

Producing Your Own CDs: A Handbook by Christian W. Huber (softcover, 6 x 9, 112 pages, $14.95)

Pro Tools Clinic: Demystifying LE for Macintosh and PC by Mitch Gallagher (softcover with CD, 448 pages, $39.95)

Apple Soundtrack Clinic: A Musician's Guide by Emile Menasché (softcover, 7 x 10, 192 pages, $18.95)

FILM STUDIES

The Independent Film Producer's Survival Guide: A Business and Legal Sourcebook (softcover, 9 x 12, 300 pages, $34.95) *New Edition Available as of January 2005*

MUSIC HISTORY

Beethoven, 2nd edition by Maynard Solomon (softcover, 6 x 9, 554 pages, $19.95)

Soulsville USA: The Story of Stax Records by Rob Bowman (softcover, 6.25 x 9.25, 416 pages, $19.95)

That's Alright, Elvis: The Untold Story of Elvis's First Guitarist and Manager, Scotty Moore by Scotty Moore as told to James Dickerson (softcover, 6 x 9, 272 pages, $19.95)

The Day the Music Died: The Last Tour of Buddy Holly, The Big Bopper, and Richie Valens by Larry Lehmer (softcover, 6.25 x 9.5, 300 pages, $17.95)

SONGWRITING

Writing Music for Hit Songs by Jai Josefs (softcover, 6 x 9, 200 pages, $20.00)

To learn more about other books available from Schirmer, visit **www.schirmertradebooks.com.**

To order by credit card, call toll-free 1-(800)-431-7187 or send a check or money order to Music Sales Corporation, 445 Bellvale Road, P.O. Box 572, Chester, NY 10918-0572. Include $5.00 for shipping and handling for the first book and .25 for each additional book. New York and New Jersey residents must include applicable sales tax.